thegoodwebguide

antiques & collectables

www.thegoodwebguide.co.uk

thegoodwebguide

antiques & collectables

caroline peacock

The Good Web Guide Limited • London

First Published in Great Britain in 2001 by The Good Web Guide Limited
Broadwall House, 21 Broadwall, London, SE1 9PL

www.thegoodwebguide.co.uk

Email:feedback@thegoodwebguide.co.uk

Original series concept by Steve Bailey.

Cover photo © Photodisc

10 9 8 7 6 5 4 3 2 1

A catalogue record for this book is available from the British Library.

ISBN 1-903282-21-7

Project Editor Michelle Clare

Design by Myriad Creative Ltd

Printed in Italy at LEGO S.p.A.

contents

the good web guides

The World Wide Web is a vast resource, with millions of sites on every conceivable subject. There are people who have made it their mission to surf the net: cyber-communities have grown, and people have formed relationships and even married on the net.

However, the reality for most people is that they don't have the time or inclination to surf the net for hours on end. Busy people want to use the internet for quick access to information. You don't have to spend hours on the internet looking for answers to your questions and you don't have to be an accomplished net surfer or cyber wizard to get the most out of the web. It can be a quick and useful resource if you are looking for specific information.

The Good Web Guides have been published with this in mind. To give you a head start in your search, our researchers have looked at hundreds of sites and what you will find in the Good Web Guides is a collection of reviews of the best we've found.

The Good Web Guide recommendation is impartial and all the sites have been visited several times. Reviews are focused on the website and what it sets out to do, rather than an endorsement of a company, or their product. A small but beautiful site run by a one-man band may be rated higher than an ambitious but flawed site run by a mighty organisation.

Relevance to the UK-based visitor is also given a high premium: tantalising as it is to read about purchases you can make in California, because of delivery charges, import duties and controls it may not be as useful as a local site.

Our reviewers considered a number of questions when reviewing the sites, such as: How quickly do the sites and individual pages download? Can you move around the site easily and get back to where you started, and do the links work? Is the information up to date and accurate? And is the site pleasing to the eye and easy to read? More importantly, we also asked whether the site has something distinctive to offer, whether it be entertainment, inspiration or pure information. On the basis of the answers to these questions sites are given ratings out of five. As we aim only to include sites that we feel are of serious interest, there are very few low-rated sites.

Bear in mind that the collection of reviews you see here is just a snapshot of the sites at a particular time. The process of choosing and writing about sites is rather like painting the Forth Bridge: as each section appears complete, new sites are launched and others are modified. When you've registered at the Good Web Guide site you can check out the reviews of new sites and updates of existing ones, or even have them emailed to you. By registering at our site, you'll find hot links to all the sites listed, so you can just click and go without needing to type the addresses accurately into your browser.

All our sites have been reviewed by the author and research team, but we'd like to know what you think. Contact us via the website or email feedback@thegoodwebguide.co.uk. You are welcome to recommend sites, quibble about the ratings, point out changes and inaccuracies or suggest new features to assess.

You can find us at www.thegoodwebguide.co.uk

introduction

The purpose of this Guide is to help those who want to make use of the internet, perhaps for the first time, to find out about antiques. There are many reasons why people get bitten by the antique collecting 'bug.' Sometimes it is merely a chance acquisition or a recently received gift that sparks our interest. We want to find out more. Numerous questions immediately come to mind: How was this thing made? Who made it? Why was it made? What purpose did it serve? How old is it? What was the social and historical context of the period to which it belonged? Are there others like it? Has it any value?

In the past, the only route to finding out the answers to these questions was either to consult an expert in person, by taking the treasured object to a museum or to a knowledgeable dealer, or to look up the information in books. Now there is what we might call 'the third way.' There is the internet.

The internet is a vast, sprawling, chaotic information resource, not unlike a library except that its 'books' are not neatly arranged on shelves or catalogued in card-indexes. Instead, it's as if they're piled high from floor to ceiling, in no particular order and with new ones being thrown in on top every day. They range, moreover, from highly relevant, academically reliable sources to completely unprofessional (though perhaps very interesting) contributions from private individuals. To find our way around, and pick out the information about antiques, or indeed about any other subject, we need help.

Help comes from search engines, which contain 'spiders' or robots computer-programmed to match documents to requests. When you put a request, perhaps the word 'antiques', into a search engine, it goes off and looks for every document - or web-page - that seems to answer that request. The problem is that search engines don't operate with any intelligence. They try to present you with what seem the best matches first, which probably means that they manage to pick out those documents where the word 'antiques' appears most frequently, but they don't have the capacity to order the answers in any more sophisticated way. They do, however, operate with incomprehensibly impressive speed. In fact, at the time of writing this Guide, the search engine Google takes 0.62 seconds to produce over a million and a half matches for the word 'antiques.' By next week it will produce more, not just a few more, probably hundreds more.

This is where the Good Web Guides come in. In writing this book, I (like any of the Good Web Guides' authors) have searched through many hundreds of websites to pick out those that contain good, clear information about the topic in question, in this case antiques and collectables. I have listed what I consider to be the best ones, and said why they are useful, and I have dismissed many more without listing them here. Even so, I have obviously not been able to look at all one and a half million. There may be some really good ones that I have missed, though I hope not many. If there are, there is a way to put this right. You can email Good Web Guides and make suggestions of other websites for inclusion in future updates, so please don't hesitate to contribute. The idea of making these regular updates available online is a feature of all the Good Web Guides, taking advantage of the interactive possibilities of this wonderful tool, the internet.

Caroline Peacock, June 2001

the online world of antiques

What does the word 'antique' mean at the beginning of the twenty-first century? At one time, not so long ago, it meant objects dating from before 1850, though any such date must necessarily move forward over time. Today the Antique Dealers' Association, LAPADA, takes the date 1910 as one benchmark, yet we find that Miller's Antiques Price Guide lists some items from as recently as the 1960s. Certainly, there is no convenient cut-off date, before which things are considered antique and after which they are merely old.

Similarly, what is an antique and what is a collectable (or 'collectible')? If it is no longer a question of age, it may be a question partly of size and partly of value. Furniture, certainly, seems to be generally accepted as being outside the range of collectables, presumably being considered too large. Value, on the other hand, does not offer a helpful distinction. Miller's Antiques Price Guide includes items that can still be bought for a few pounds, while the parallel Collectables Guide contains a few that fetch four-figure sums, certainly putting them beyond the reach of most average collectors.

Next there are replicas, reproductions and, regrettably, fakes to consider. Strictly speaking, a replica should have been made by the original artist, though this definition is increasingly disregarded and the terms 'replica' and 'reproduction' tend to be used almost interchangeably. Meanwhile, to complicate things further, there are plenty of businesses blithely advertising furniture or other objects newly made to old designs as 'antiques made by our highly-skilled craftsmen', an obvious nonsense. The issue of whether or not an object is genuine is one that worries all collectors, and it is even more worrying when you read some

of the stories recounted by certain websites listed here. For instance, there is an item in the Antiques World website warning collectors about faked ceramic 'authenticity tags' on teddy bears. Fakers will go to great lengths to dupe collectors, whom they see as easy prey, and only years of experience will help collectors get the better of them.

So why, with all this to worry about, would you even consider buying antiques over the internet? After all, you would be buying things that you had possibly not even seen (since many items are offered for sale without a photograph to support the written description) and you would certainly be buying objects that you had not handled. In the case of the online auctioneers, you would be buying from a range of completely unknown dealers and private individuals, with no knowledge of their expertise or honesty. It is true that these auctioneers mostly compile credit records of all those who buy and sell through their websites, and are admirably up-front about publishing any complaints received, but that is all the reassurance you get.

Nevertheless, before you decide that this is all too perilous and you don't want to get involved, look also at the advantages. The usefulness of Ebay and similar auction websites, as well as those of the multitudinous dealers who advertise on the internet, lies in the 'breadth' of the audience. As a buyer, you get access to thousands more sources than you could ever possibly visit in person. As a seller, you reach vastly greater numbers of prospective purchasers than you could ever entice to your shop or similar outlet.

This vastly enlarged pool of buyers and sellers has obvious uses if you are interested in a collecting field where you can identify very clearly the precise items that will make your own collection more complete. Sometimes, those items can be quite small and quite inexpensive, but they may be of huge value to the collector. You might, for instance, be collecting King Penguin books. Only a limited number were ever published, some of which are not hard to find, some of which are scarce, and one or two of which are hardly ever found. The internet would be a perfect tool for tracking down those elusive volumes that would complete your set, and the correct items would be so clearly identifiable as genuine that, provided you paid attention to the description of the books' condition, you should not be in danger of being 'done'.

One reason why ceramics is such a popular field for trading online is, again, that many ceramics items are clearly identifiable. A Susie Cooper poppy design cup and saucer, for example, is unmistakable and it is very unlikely that you would be offered a fake. Once identification comes down to personal judgement, however, rather than any recognised marks, you may feel less secure about buying. This, of course, is the same problem that faces the collector who finds an apparently desirable object in a shop - except that in that situation you can handle the item, which gives you another method by which to judge its authenticity. Buying over the internet, you do take a certain amount on trust. On the other hand, you can normally return items that don't meet your expectations, so you probably end up with about as good a level of guarantee as you might get from the average dealer in the high street.

Even if you decide not to buy online, the internet can still be a wonderfully useful resource. Let's say you wish to decorate your bedroom in Japanese style, or you would like to fill a display cabinet with Art Deco crockery, how can you find out where to go and look for such things? The internet has the answer. Put the words 'oriental lacquerware' or 'art deco' into a search engine, remembering to add 'UK' if you want to find dealers in this country, press the return button on your keyboard or click 'search', and the answers will be in front of you in seconds. Now you know where to telephone or where to travel to pursue your quest. No method of equivalent efficiency for putting buyers in touch with sellers, or vice versa, has ever existed before.

There is a view, certainly, that this new marketplace has attracted large numbers of cynical dealers who are buying not out of interest or enthusiasm for the objects themselves but simply in order to re-sell them at a profit, thereby raising prices at an artificially rapid rate. I am not personally convinced that this is the case and, anyway, it could be argued that, conversely, the increased competition is more likely to keep prices down. Perhaps, in fact, the very price-conscious approach to the world of antiques collecting has been fostered much more by television than by the internet.

Finally, I come to the criteria by which I have judged the antiques and collectables websites listed in the following pages. I must make it very clear that I have not included websites that are simply shop windows. For a start, it won't be long before every antique shop in the country has an online presence of this sort, so it would be impossible to list them all. In any case, dealers are very easy indeed to find through any search engine and their websites are seldom at all complicated to use. In order to qualify for inclusion here, therefore, a website - even if it is principally a dealer's online 'showroom' - must also offer good informative material about a specialist field of antiques or collecting. My objective is to help collectors use the internet to learn about antiques, rather than merely find them.

This proviso actually cuts down dramatically the number of websites that could qualify for inclusion. It is surprising, and disappointing, how little information is available to collectors in relation to the vast numbers of items being sold. Here and there, though, you will find splendidly clear and helpful information being given online. You can read some fascinating articles about the history and background of the objects you collect, along with advice about what to look for in choosing the best examples, and about how to care for them. This is good, practical advice and, if you feel you still need to know more, you can also access excellent lists of books that will expand your knowledge further.

One little word of warning here: you can, and often should, arrange insurance for your collection too. Do be somewhat wary, however, of inviting valuers to your home unless you are very certain of their respectability. There have been too many cases of in-the-home valuations being followed disturbingly soon by burglaries, so it may be safer to take your collection to the valuer, if possible, instead. There are now a few online valuation services, notably Hugh Scully's (see p.41), and this depends on photographs supported by verbal descriptions. Such valuations are, of course, a guide only.

Another way of increasing your knowledge about the items you are collecting is, of course, to visit museums, galleries and stately homes where antiques are displayed. I have not included lists of these sources here because, again, it is not hard to find them by means of fairly simple online searches. In any case, there is now a Good Web Guide to Museums & Galleries that would make an excellent companion to this book for any serious collector.

Similarly, an entire book could be dedicated to art, meaning fine art, on the internet as opposed to antiques. This book does not attempt to cover that ground either, although you will find that fine art may appear incidentally, as a result of sharing website space with antiques. Anyone who wants to explore this field further could start with a good fine art journal, such as 'Art Review' (www.art-review.co.uk) or 'Galleries' (www.artefact.co.uk).

The pattern throughout the Good Web Guides series is to award websites star-ratings for content, reliability, ease of navigation and speed, and then give each one an overall rating as well. It might seem a difficult task to assess websites in this way and I can confidently assure you that all the websites here are worth consulting anyway, regardless of their star-ratings. Nevertheless, when the really good ones come up they stand out a mile! It is the pattern also to list the five-star sites first, then the four-star ones and so on, and only to sort them alphabetically within those bands.

For advice about the techniques of using search engines, please turn to the introduction to Part Two of this Guide on p.51. I hope you will find much to enjoy in this book and will spend happy, but also productive and rewarding hours online, using these websites to further your knowledge and appreciation of the wonderful world of antiques and antiques-collecting.

user key

 £   Subscription

 R   Registration Required

     Secure Online Ordering

 UK   Country of Origin

Chapter 01

general gateways

The first section of this Guide is devoted to those websites that cover a great deal of ground, from which you can pursue almost any collecting interest. These are big websites, information-rich and full of advice for collectors. Because they are so densely packed, however, finding your way around may be a little complicated. Usually the best policy is simply to explore any links that look interesting, and see what you find. That is, unless you are seeking information about something very specific, in which case you may be able to specify your request in a search box and short-cut to the right information straight away.

In general, these websites will offer you a mix of information, ranging from details of forthcoming exhibitions and events (including auctions) to lists of dealers nationwide, and articles on various collecting interests by experts. They will probably also tell you how to access valuation advice, how to insure your property, what you can do to try and recover stolen goods and so on. They may publish their own leaflets or magazines, or even offer books. What they seek to be, in fact, is libraries of information about everything to do with antiques and collecting.

The first eight websites listed here all earn five-star ratings, so I really would urge you to make use of all of them very regularly, at least to begin with. They do not, in fact, duplicate each other greatly in terms of the information they provide. You will soon identify which are the most useful in terms of your own particular collecting interests, and any that prove especially helpful you can eventually store in your 'bookmarks' or 'favorites' folder.

http://ukantiques.about.com
Antiques: UK

Overall rating: ★ ★ ★ ★ ★			
Classification:	General	Readability:	★ ★ ★ ★ ★
Updating:	Regularly	Reliability:	★ ★ ★ ★
Navigation:	★ ★ ★ ★	Speed:	★ ★ ★ ★ ★

UK

Carol Fisher is the antiques enthusiast and writer who hosts this UK-based, antiques-related portal as part of the sizeable search engine, About.com. A click on 'become a partner' leads to the information about the Luna partnership which recruits website contributors and apparently turns down all but about 10% of applicants, which certainly should ensure high standards.

SPECIAL FEATURES

The homepage presentation is fairly busy, betraying the website's American influences, but it is still thoroughly usable. The collecting subject index fills the margin to the left of the page, while special features, including forthcoming antiques fairs, occupies the centre of the page. Under **Related Sites** on the right hand are links to other people's websites. **Book Collecting**, for example, leads eventually to a booksearch application hosted by Addall. These onward links are too numerous to detail here, so the best advice is simply explore....

In the subject index some of the more general articles are rewarding, such as Buying On-line or Care of Antiques, though the standard of presentation varies widely. Golfiana is one of the collecting fields listed, not found in every such list by any means.

Recent Articles, in the bar below the grey page-header, is

definitely an area to explore. **Forums** was still under development, but **Chat Live** enables you to 'speak' to other UK-based enthusiasts online at 8pm on Thursdays. **Contact Guide** offers an email facility where you can seek or offer advice and suggestions, though it is made clear that this is not a means of seeking valuations. **Free Newsletters** allows you to subscribe simply by clicking on the 'subscribe' button and then filling in an email contact address. A list of other **About Guides** is then offered, as well as **Antiques: UK Newsletter**. A bit more information about what an issue might contain would be more enticing.

Finally, don't ignore the search box in the centre of the grey header-bar that appears on every page. This works well, the word 'barometers' producing one good link from within the Antiques part of this website and 164 from the About network as a whole. Some of these, admittedly, used the term generically, as in 'barometers of trends', but the majority were very relevant, covering everything from the history and science of barometers, to their inventors and today's restorers.

This is an impressively well organised, rapid-to-use website, containing a vast amount of information. It would be a good first port of call for any collecting topic.

www.antiquesworld.co.uk
Antiques World

Overall rating: ★ ★ ★ ★

Classification:	General	Readability:	★ ★ ★ ★ ★
Updating:	Regular	Reliability:	★ ★ ★ ★
Navigation:	★ ★ ★ ★ ★	Speed:	★ ★ ★ ★ ★

UK

The subtitle tells it all: The leading UK directory of information for everyone with an interest, private or professional, in antiques and collectables. The homepage could be made less cluttered, however, by making use of the blank column space that occupies the right of the page.

SPECIAL FEATURES

The left-of-page index is divided into four categories: **Editorial** contains both Features by Experts, on such varied topics as Baxter Prints, Cruise Liner Keepsakes, Perfume Bottles and Railway Ephemera, and Book Reviews, covering a similarly wide list of subjects. **Publications** offers Books, a link to a handful of specialist publishers, and Magazines, which lists all the major journals with contact details for each and a two-line explanation of contents.

Organisations heads a longer list that begins with Collectors' Clubs, currently starting with the Alton Bottle Collectors' Club (Hampshire) boasting 22 members and ending with The Writing Equipment Society boasting 600. Then follow Dealers & Trade, Restoration & Conservation, and Research & Education, all self-explanatory. These are good lists, though by no means exhaustive, as is evident from the fact that only nine Research and Education Organisations are so far included. Many more must exist. **Museums & Art Galleries**, a link to a list maintained by the Royal Academy of Arts, suffers from the same problem.

Events lists Major Fairs, Local Fairs & Markets and Major Exhibitions, all most useful. **Antiques Tours** links to one specialist operator, In the Limelight, a Wiltshire-based company offering tours by coach, rail and air to Belgium, the Czech Republic, France, Holland, Ireland and the UK at apparently reasonable prices. Finally **Study Courses** gives a good list including many reputable providers such as The Courtauld Institute, NADFAS (The National Association of Design and Fine Art Societies), the Victoria and Albert Museum and West Dean College.

Finally, at the bottom of the index column is a search facility, headed Find. Testing this with 'caddy spoons' brought up the name of a specialist collecting group whose address was listed as lost, although a request for information to restore it was posted, a sensible approach. 'Scrimshaw', which produced no information from within the Antiques World website itself, offered a link to the search engine Look Smart, and that had several good and relevant links.

This is an exemplary website full of well-ordered information, certainly of value to the serious collector.

www.artworlddealers.com
Art World Dealers

Overall rating: ★ ★ ★ ★ ★			
Classification:	General	**Readability:**	★ ★ ★ ★ ★
Updating:	Regular	**Reliability:**	★ ★ ★ ★
Navigation:	★ ★ ★ ★ ★	**Speed:**	★ ★ ★ ★ ★

BE

An impressive international directory of main players in the fine art world. See About Us, lower left of the homepage, for a further explanation.

Use the tabs at the top of the page to get started. The total index of dealers in fine art worldwide is organised alphabetically by Names, then by Cities (countries, followed by cities, in fact), then by Specialities. Fairs are listed by the month, with details of exhibitors who will be present. Associations are listed alphabetically, some with onward links to their own websites.

SPECIAL FEATURES

The Art World is almost useful area of the website, offering Art Press, with a mass of onward links to media dealing with art matters; Auction Houses (which lists only the London big four); Art Resources, another good list of websites; Art Data, websites through which to track auction and sale prices; Appraisal, suggesting who to contact; Insurance & Law, also with a brief list of online resources; and Museums, another good list of online links to explore.

The homepage has a few other areas to entice you, not least **Art Tour**, which gives you a virtual tour of the Xavier Hufkens gallery in Belgium. It takes a little time to load and requires the QuickTime plug-in, which is available free, provided you have enough RAM.

Note: a useful shortcut for picking out the British-based websites is to use the 'Edit' button at the top of your screen, select 'Find (on this page)' and then enter 'UK' in the search box provided. This will highlight all appearances of the letters 'UK' throughout the text, including all those instances where the URL ends '.co.uk', a quicker route than reading through the entire list. You will find that you can still scroll the page behind the search-window normally.

A very stylish website doing something admirably simple, well.

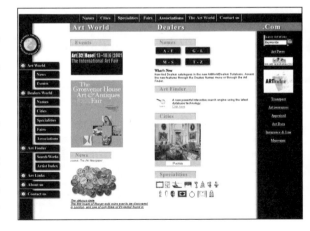

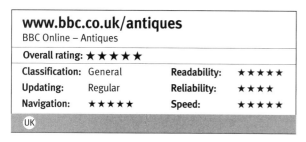

www.bbc.co.uk/antiques
BBC Online – Antiques

Overall rating: ★ ★ ★ ★			
Classification:	General	Readability:	★ ★ ★ ★ ★
Updating:	Regular	Reliability:	★ ★ ★ ★
Navigation:	★ ★ ★ ★ ★	Speed:	★ ★ ★ ★ ★

UK

The BBC's own Antiques website approaches the subject in an attractive, entertaining and user-friendly way, and is a good starting point for anyone venturing into the antiques world on the web for the first time.

At the top of the left-hand menu, there's a link called 'Antiques'; note that this is the page that you're actually on.

SPECIAL FEATURES

Roadshow Finds features some of the items that have been brought to recent Antiques Roadshow events, divided under ten headings including Furniture, Jewellery, and Pictures and Prints. In most instances the valuations given by the experts are listed, along with some comments, and the majority of items are well illustrated. Pictures can be enlarged by a single click.

Antique of the Week is typically a single page of information about a particular collecting topic. The **Quiz** feature is only periodically open to contestants. **What's On** leads to a page that duplicates some of the links in the homepage menu under Features, Buyers' Guides and Specialist Guides. Under **Experts,** you will find a list of the various advisers to the programme, all with thumbnail portraits and brief details. Note that the first page covers only those with surnames beginning A to E; there are three further pages to look at. The Feature Articles are clear and informative.

Know How is divided into Clubs and Societies, Valuation Advice, Bibliography and Links. There is also a link to a **Hallmarks Guide**, for those wishing to identify silver marks. If working your way through the homepage index for the first time, you will probably now find it more logical to click on **Tricks,** which is the last item listed. This is a useful list of tips on how to repair broken or damaged articles.

Message Board offers four interactive facilities, Antiques Bargains (questions to the experts), The Virtual Sofa (home decoration advice-swapping), Nuts and Bolts (DIY advice) and Inspirational Ideas. You won't learn all that much more about antiques here, though some of the items people describe are intriguing. To contribute to (rather than just read) this area of the website you need to register and then log in. The process is very simple, merely a matter of giving a name, an email address and a password.

Finally, if you click on **My BBC** you will be transported away from the Antiques area altogether, to recent national news items; whereas oddly enough, clicking on Feedback does keep you, loosely speaking, in the world of antiques, because it gives you the opportunity to respond to an invitation that reads 'Got something to say? This is the place to say it' and then offers you the chance to contribute a question to the Antiques quiz.

Absolutely no contest, this is one of the best.

www.collectiques.co.uk
Collectiques

Overall rating: ★ ★ ★ ★ ★

Classification:	General	**Readability:**	★ ★ ★ ★ ★
Updating:	Regular	**Reliability:**	★ ★ ★ ★
Navigation:	★ ★ ★ ★ ★	**Speed:**	★ ★ ★ ★ ★

UK

A general portal or gateway into the world of collecting, concentrating mainly on smaller or less expensive items but still addressing antiques too.

SPECIAL FEATURES

Look under **Collectors Directory** to see what areas of the website you could explore. The categories range from Archaeology to Toys & Games, and each category is subdivided into specific collecting interests. Clicking on any topic produces a selection of pages, many of which are links to dealers, though often there is some general information too. The little flags alongside each link are a convenient way of indicating national origin for the websites concerned. Even clicking on one of these will probably not have exhausted your options – there are links and sub-links to explore throughout this website.

This is a true collectors' directory, well organised and very easy to use.

www.cornucopi.org.uk
Cornucopia – Discovering UK Collections

Overall rating: ★ ★ ★ ★ ★

Classification:	Small collections	**Readability:**	★ ★ ★ ★ ★
Updating:	Regular	**Reliability:**	★ ★ ★ ★ ★
Navigation:	★ ★ ★ ★	**Speed:**	★ ★ ★ ★ ★

UK

When it comes to the business of identifying where obscure collections (they call them 'the pre-eminent Designated Collections'), especially of things like scientific instruments, are to be found, no website can beat Cornucopia.

This amazing website is dedicated to knowledge, and it does one very simple thing, very well. It seeks out the specialist collections nationwide and allows you to interrogate them by Objects & Collections, by Museums, by People (artist, maker, donor) or by Places (worldwide). Say, for instance, you were interested to find out where there might be an orrery exhibited, Cornucopia will tell you. The earliest English orrery, it turns out, was made by Thomas Tompion and George Graham and is in the Oxford University Museum of the History of Science, while there is another exhibited in the Whipple Museum of the History of Science at the University of Cambridge.

SPECIAL FEATURES

The **Picture Gallery** offers thumbnail pictures, which can all be enlarged by clicking, from each of the Museums listed. It is intriguing to see what the various museums have chosen as landmark or definitive objects. The Ashmolean, for instance, selects its own facade (by Cockerell), the Alfred Jewel, part of a 14th century BC fresco depicting the daughters of Akhenaten and Nefertiti, and a drawing of an angel by Raphael.

This website is not illustrated nor does it even give website links to the museums or holdings identified, but it does tell you what is to be found where – an invaluable service.

If you are looking for something a little obscure and the location of such an object is difficult to identify, come here and you will almost certainly find it. So valuable is this service that it earns a five-star rating despite its relatively limited aspirations design-wise.

www.lapada.co.uk
LAPADA – The Association of Art and Antiques Dealers

Overall rating: ★ ★ ★ ★ ★			
Classification:	General	**Readability:**	★ ★ ★ ★ ★
Updating:	Regular	**Reliability:**	★ ★ ★ ★
Navigation:	★ ★ ★ ★ ★	**Speed:**	★ ★ ★ ★ ★

UK

This elegant website provides LAPADA with a forum to showcase their 700 members, from the UK and beyond.

SPECIAL FEATURES

The first link in the menu led to the website's search facility. Tested with the word 'Treen', it produced a list of a dozen dealers, selected on the basis that the same word is mentioned in their own brief descriptions of their stock. **About LAPADA** is self explanatory, while **News and Information** offers you the chance to receive the Association's own magazine, 'News & Views' by email.

Membership lists dealers geographically by county, then by town and finally by name. The list is restricted to members, of course, so this can unbalance the picture. In York, for instance, only two dealers are listed, neither of them actually in the city. This would imply that York is not a good hunting ground for antiques collectors, something that is by no means the case. **Fairs & Shows** lists LAPADA's own events first and then, from a link at the bottom of that page headed **Diary of Art and Antique Fairs,** a reasonable number of other events around the country. **Buying & Selling** produces a page of general advice, with left-of-margin links to further help under headings such as Buying in London, Buying at Fairs and Selling Antiques.

Useful Links includes Associations (many of which are foreign), Loss Registers and Police Contacts (which provide information about recovery of stolen works of art and antiques), and Publications (a list of magazines rather than books).

Services leads to advice about the regulations governing the export of antiques. Again, onward links offer more advice, about such things as Valuations and Restoration, as well as LAPADA's very worthwhile Conciliation service, which may be of help in cases of dispute between purchaser and dealer. LAPADA gift vouchers, available in denominations of £50 or £100, might be the ideal solution to a tricky present-giving problem.

Care of Antiques has good advice about security, as well as practical information about cleaning and conservation (including the suggestion that you seal the backs of pictures with gummed tape to 'keep our (sic) dust and insects'). **Publications** lists and describes only LAPADA's own two titles, 'Buying Antiques in Britain 1999/2000' and 'Buying and Selling Art and Antiques – The Law.' In the left-of-page index, however, there is a link to Care Leaflets, four of which address conservation methods while four more give details of regional associations. These are free of charge.

Definitely a gilt-edged website in terms of its presentation, with good practical information and rapid responses.

www.worldcollectorsnet.com
World Collectors Net

Overall rating: ★ ★ ★ ★ ★			
Classification: General		**Readability:**	★ ★ ★ ★
Updating: Regular		**Reliability:**	★ ★ ★ ★
Navigation: ★ ★ ★ ★ ★		**Speed:**	★ ★ ★ ★ ★

UK

A good general starting point for anyone 'into' collectables, mainly thanks to the great breadth of information and the well-organised layout. This claims to be the largest collectables content site in the world.

SPECIAL FEATURES

Collections Featured lists nearly 100 collecting fields containing everything from Caithness Glass to Barbie Dolls, and from Calico Kittens to Wizards & Dragons. **OnLine Magazine** claims to come out monthly and in January a message wishing all readers a Happy New Year seemed appropriate enough. Clicking on 'back issues', however, reveals that publication has been somewhat erratic, with every two months appearing a more normal frequency. Even so, the articles are interesting and well-illustrated, with pictures that load rapidly, and there is also a regular competition.

Links Directory leads to another excellent list, including some invaluable websites that help you track down discontinued lines of china tableware.

With one of the most impressive lists of collectables categories, and a host of links accordingly, this has to be worth some of your time.

www.antiquesbulletin.com
Antiques Bulletin Online

Overall rating: ★ ★ ★ ★			
Classification:	General	**Readability:**	★ ★ ★ ★
Updating:	Regular	**Reliability:**	★ ★ ★ ★
Navigation:	★ ★ ★ ★	**Speed:**	★ ★ ★

UK US

Despite its title, which suggests some sort of online e-zine, Antiques Bulletin is actually a general gateway website. It offers a slightly strange mix of information, where details of antiques fairs simultaneously being held in California, Monaco and Derby (UK) may all be found in a single list. It rewards a bit of investigation, however, and in general the emphasis is towards the UK.

The first decision is whether to view with or without frames. Assuming your browser can view frames, you get a more complete version of the website if you select that option. The non-framed version might be preferred, by anyone who dislikes small print.

There's a simple menu to the left of the homepage with links to Auctions, Fairs, Dealers, Services and so on, which work well, though the large banners that part-fill each page leave little room for new information and scrolling on the toolbar is invariably necessary.

SPECIAL FEATURES

Info offers nine boxes, some of which require subscription for entry. Among these, Art Prices Index is open to all and is a good way of finding recent prices fetched at auction. To understand the entries you need to print out a key to the abbreviations used. Even using this, you will find that details of individual works are limited and prices are not always prefixed by a currency indicator, which is puzzling. With more detail, and pictures, this facility would be really useful. **Book Reviews** is also available to all, and is well done – though if the list gets much longer some sort of division into categories will be needed.

Buy and Sell offers a free service for advertising items for sale and listing items wanted. The **Library** is a most useful area of the website, offering a good range of specialist articles. These are then accessed by clicking on the topics in the index, where the print is unfortunately annoyingly small. **Publications** offers Antiques Magazine (see also p.28), The Antiques Fairs and Centres Guide, Pine World and Antiques Companion, each on their own independent websites. Bookstore was still under construction at the time of writing.

Disentangling things on this website can take a little time, but the information itself is good.

www.antiques-info.co.uk
Antiques Information Services

Overall rating: ★ ★ ★ ★			
Classification: General		**Readability:**	★ ★ ★ ★ ★
Updating: Regular		**Reliability:**	★ ★ ★ ★
Navigation: ★ ★ ★ ★		**Speed:**	★ ★ ★
UK			

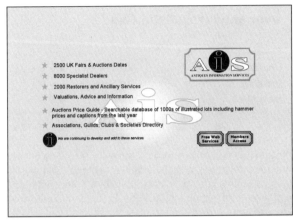

A guide to Auctions (with a database of last year's results) and Fairs, specialist dealers, restorers, valuers and associations. Full access is restricted to members.

SPECIAL FEATURES

Click on **Free Web Services** to view the parts of the website that are open to all. **Fairs and Auctions** offer lists for the coming week throughout the UK, though even with that limitation on dates the number of events listed is considerable.

News Service is densely informative and seems to be kept well up to date, warning about such things as recently stolen items and fakes, as well as giving more general news such as information about Sotheby's new saleroom at Olympia, and details of recent auctions, forthcoming events, courses and the like. **Prize Competitions** offers a monthly prize crossword and a £50 first prize, with smaller runners-up prizes, or a single question to answer to win a year's subscription (worth £24) to the Gold Service. Advisory and valuation services are only available to Gold Service members, and the relevant button appears on every page.

The blue **Magazine** button does not appear on all pages. Clicking on it leads to a page headed Antiques Info Magazine, describing it as 'the leading informational source on the UK antiques and collecting industry.' Reading the list

of typical topics covered, and the few readers' comments alongside, might encourage you to click on How to Subscribe, the only live link on the page. Here, some sample covers are shown, various offers on the basic subscription of £15.60 for a year (six issues) are made, and an online subscription form is given.

A bit more online information about the content of Antiques Info Magazine might be helpful, but the rest of the site is well constructed and the distinction between what members and non-members can access is fair and clearly explained.

www.antiquestree.co.uk
Antiques Tree UK

Overall rating: ★ ★ ★ ★			
Classification:	General	Readability:	★ ★ ★ ★
Updating:	Regular	Reliability:	★ ★ ★
Navigation:	★ ★ ★ ★	Speed:	★ ★ ★

UK

This is a good general directory, presented in a very simple manner. Don't expect much information, though. It is mainly of use as an introduction to specialist dealers.

The mustard-coloured homepage is one of the simplest you will find, with an alphabetical list of collecting categories. Click on any of these and you will be taken to a list of specialist dealers, some of whom are trading exclusively online.

SPECIAL FEATURES

The **News Section** link, incidentally, is disappointing in that it only leads to current, general news items, not features especially related to antiques and collecting. Much more helpful is **Collectors Reference**, which leads to some genuinely informative links, even though the great majority focus on porcelain and pottery. Another link, **Collectors Magazines**, contained only four items at the time of writing. There is also a **Wants Page**, where you can fill in details of any particular collecting field or item you are interested in.

For anyone approaching the use of the internet for the first time, this is a simple, clear starting point.

www.antiquesweb.co.uk
Antiquesweb

Overall rating: ★ ★ ★ ★			
Classification:	General	Readability:	★ ★ ★ ★ ★
Updating:	Daily	Reliability:	★ ★ ★ ★
Navigation:	★ ★ ★ ★	Speed:	★ ★ ★ ★

UK

This agreeably straightforward website offers half a dozen tabs at the top of the page to guide you around. Latest additions are listed in the left-of-page margin. Don't confuse this website with Antique Web (www.antiqueweb.co.uk), which is a Lancashire-based website promoting dealers, fairs and other events, mainly in the North West of England.

SPECIAL FEATURES

Showrooms offers several categories under which you can view items for sale. On the occasions tested, some categories contained items from only one dealer, and others no items at all. As the site attracts users, however, the range of goods will presumably expand. **Dealers** offers a map from which to select an area, and then a list of counties. Clicking on one of these produces the names of local businesses. **Auction Guide** features the next two months' forthcoming auctions. Auction dates illuminate when you click on them, with Saturdays being the most popular. **Fairs Guide** operates in exactly the same way. **News** contains short articles posted by web-owner Amy Schofield.

A well-organised, though not huge, website that earns a good star-rating for clarity as much as content.

www.icollectit.co.uk				
I Collect It				
Overall rating: ★ ★ ★ ★				
Classification:	General	**Readability:**		★ ★ ★
Updating:	Regular	**Reliability:**		★ ★ ★
Navigation:	★ ★ ★ ★	**Speed:**		★ ★ ★ ★
UK				

About Us, at the bottom of each page, explains more about how this website is put together and what its ultimate objectives are, namely to create 'the best site for UK collectors but with links around the planet.'

SPECIAL FEATURES

If you were to judge solely from the left-margin index, you would assume this to be a website only for those collecting at the very 'economical' end of the market. The list starts with Action Figures and includes Cigarette Cards, Comics, Models and Telephone Cards. It also contains **Books and Stamps**, however, two collecting interests with long pedigrees, on which you can spend very serious money. Clicking on any of these topics will produce a handful of introductory articles, followed by details of any forthcoming fairs and events (a further click needed), and then links to dealers.

To participate by adding an article, to use the search facility or to take part in the interactive areas of the website, you have to register. The facility for this is available from the right-of-page index.

This is one of those websites where you just have to plunge in and start rummaging around. Its charm lies partly in its quirkiness, since the contributors are all individuals with the collecting bug, so who knows what you may find?

www.bbc.co.uk/antiques/antiques roadshow				
Antiques Roadshow				
Overall rating: ★ ★ ★ ★				
Classification:	General	**Readability:**		★ ★ ★ ★
Updating:	Regular	**Reliability:**		★ ★ ★ ★
Navigation:	★ ★ ★	**Speed:**		★ ★
UK				

The famous BBC television programme, its format now copied worldwide, has its own website here. Don't confuse it with the American version.

There are two ways to navigate this site: either via the menu on the left-hand side of the page, or through the picture features (all of which have their own links). Though this may be an unnecessary duplication, it is worth persisting, in order to explore the information behind. Incidentally, don't click on BBC Homepage or Homes unless you want to get transported away from Antiques altogether.

SPECIAL FEATURES

Roadshow Finds describes the objects brought before the programme's experts for evaluation. A short list of categories, such as Ceramics and Glass, or Jewellery, is headed by the option 'Latest Programme'. Clicking on this link, without filling in the search box at the foot of the page, brings up a list of all the items shown in the most recent programme, each of which can then be viewed individually. **Antique of the Week** is a short feature about a special object, usually soon to be sold. An example was the embroidered cap said to have been worn by King Charles I to his execution, a relic expected to fetch as much as £50,000 at a forthcoming Christie's sale (subsequently found to have been sold, in fact, for only £23,500).

Quiz produces a new window in which a series of ten questions is posed. It appears somewhat slow both to ask the questions and produce the answers, so is probably best explored only if you have time to spare. **Exhibitions** highlights a small selection of those exhibitions taking place in the current week, giving a brief description of each and contact details. **What's On**, however, links to details of BBC programmes on radio and TV, often with only tenuous links to antiques as a topic – for instance, the chance to win dinner with the Antiques Roadshow experts if you get involved with Children in Need.

Features is misleadingly subtitled 'cut glass information that will get you ahead in this collectable area'. It turns out not to be about cut glass specifically, but instead a route to a range of articles under half a dozen headings, such as Chats with the Experts, Investment and Styles & Designs. This is an area of the website that certainly rewards exploration. **Know How** also introduces a set of useful onward links, under Hallmarks Guide (help with identifying silver marks), Clubs and Societies, Valuation Advice, Bibliography, and Links. This last gives handy brief reviews of either Antiques websites or Museum and Gallery websites.

Message Board is where you can post those sticky questions that have been puzzling you for years. It makes informative reading, and it is encouraging to see that answers normally come back within days. Finally, **Tricks** is a most useful guide to the sort of minor repairs or cleaning processes you can use at home, such as getting rid of woodworm in furniture, or mending terracotta flower pots.

Speed is not one of the virtues of this website, but the information within is considerable, and reliable, so the best advice is don't give up.

www.TheAntiquesDirectory.co.uk
The Antiques Directory

Overall rating: ★ ★ ★			
Classification:	General	Readability:	★ ★ ★ ★
Updating:	Regular	Reliability:	★ ★ ★
Navigation:	★ ★ ★ ★	Speed:	★ ★ ★ ★

UK

This general gateway website covers a very wide field, which contributes both to its usefulness and, inevitably, to its limitations. Watch out when you're clicking on the links; though you are clicking through to a new page each time, you may not realise it because the upper half of each page remains the same. You need to scroll down to see the new information.

SPECIAL FEATURES

This is a clear and well designed website, offering a multiplicity of links. **Auctions & Auctioneers** offers a list of counties, though clicking on two, Durham and North Yorkshire, produced no results, which suggests the information is somewhat biased in favour of the south of England. **Books about Antiques** brings up a limited list, where clicking on the pictures of the book covers (which eventually load to the left of your screen) transports you direct to Amazon. **Fairs & Shows** again produces none in Durham or North Yorkshire. **Antiques Magazines** leads to a less than impressive list, downmarket by comparison with the list at Antiques World (see p.13) and was aimed more at collectibles than antiques.

Information is a somewhat impenetrable title, and leads to a list of collecting categories with everything from Advertising Signs to Vintage Luggage. Pursuing these links may, disappointingly, lead to purveyors of reproductions rather than the real thing. Certainly this was the case when tested with 'Sculpture'. Incidentally, these links are only available online, so that clicking rapidly simply to open them, in the hope of being able to re-visit them offline at a later time, doesn't work. The same problem with offline return visits applies to **Miscellaneous**, where categories include Carriage & Shipping, Currency Conversion, Restorers & Restoration (only one listed), Travel and Tourism (only two, and one of those is a restorer of antique luggage who presumably got into the wrong index) and Media, which is carefully subtitled 'Newspapers, Radio & TV'. This last has a useful link to Historic Newspapers at www.classicengland.co.uk. Webmaster Resources, also under the Miscellaneous link, reveals the problem with this website, and that is that contributors select their own locations for listing within the site. This presumably explains why another restorer appears under Directories but not under Restorers & Restoration.

Shops & Shopping is again limited in scope, with only one small business listed in York, for example, where of course many more could (and to make the website really useful, should) be listed. Again, the site is dependent on those shop owners who contribute their own information, and the result is inevitably patchy even though inclusion in the lists is free. Video's (sic) about Antiques looks promising but the link to one that appeared to be about Charles Rennie Mackintosh drew a blank when pursued to the individual page.

Many things about this website are good, not least the clear layout and speed of use, but the indexing would benefit from better organisation and comprehensiveness is still a long way off. This will not be resolved until either all auctioneers, restorers, shop owners, book and magazine publishers recognise the value of being listed or – perhaps more reliably – someone at The Antiques Directory makes a point of creating lists on their behalf.

OTHER SITES OF INTEREST

Collector Online
www.collectoronline.com
Though very American in presentation and content, this website covers a lot of ground in the collecting field, and is still useful for UK collectors, particularly those with an interest in Americana. Clicking on Shop the Mall on the homepage will lead you into the selling area of the website, organised into categories alphabetically, starting with Advertising Collectibles and Americana, and ending with Trading Cards and Transportation. Other options from the homepage include Read & Learn, which contains a good list of articles on collecting topics, even allowing for the very strong American slant. The other two homepage links are aimed at people selling, who may want to 'rent a booth' in the Mall.

Antiques Catalogue
www.antiques-catalogue.co.uk

Access to this site involves registration and is aimed at dealers rather than members of the general public. For a one-off registration fee, dealers gain access to, apparently, some 900 search engines worldwide. The less than attractive homepage is not immediately inviting and a lot of scrolling is involved in getting around. To get round this problem, click on Sitemap, the very last item in the left-of-page index. This produces a compressed list of contents, helpfully divided under Company, Communications and UK Antique Dealerships.

Chapter 02

journals

I have called this section 'Journals' to distinguish it from the collecting topics section that fills the latter part of this Guide, where Magazines & Periodicals appear as one of many collecting interests. The websites listed here either exist solely to deliver to their readers regular articles about antiques and collectables (whether online, on the news-stands or both) or they have that function as their principal purpose.

Being regular publications, they nearly all tell their readers about auctions or forthcoming events in the antiques world, and some of them also provide detailed lists of dealers, so in those respects they are not perhaps very different from the gateway websites in the previous section. These websites all, however, award their function as journals top billing, so to speak. In other words, delivering up-to-date news about developments in the art and antiques world is their principal objective.

In most cases they also provide lists of the articles that have appeared in their own back issues, and this can prove a rich hunting ground for knowledgeable articles on specialist topics. You may find, indeed, that this is one of their principal uses. As often as not, you will need to subscribe to receive these journals, either paying a subscription just as you would for any periodical, or at the very least filling in a form with your email address. If you are considering subscribing, and if the magazine you are considering exists in hard-copy for the news-stands, I would strongly advise you to buy a few copies and see if the type of content really answers your needs, before committing yourself.

www.atg-online.com
Antiques Trade Gazette

Overall rating: ★ ★ ★ ★ ★			
Classification:	Journal	**Readability:**	★ ★ ★ ★ ★
Updating:	★ ★ ★ ★	**Reliability:**	★ ★ ★ ★ ★
Navigation:	★ ★ ★ ★ ★	**Speed:**	★ ★ ★ ★ ★

UK

www.antiquesandart.com.au
The World of Antiques & Art

Overall rating: ★ ★ ★ ★ ★			
Classification:	Journal	**Readability**	★ ★ ★ ★ ★
Updating:	Regular	**Reliability:**	★ ★ ★ ★
Navigation:	★ ★ ★ ★ ★	**Speed:**	★ ★ ★ ★ ★

AUS

Though mainly aimed at professionals, the Antiques Trade Gazette attracts private collectors too. Its principal function is to inform about forthcoming auctions and fairs. Full access to the magazine is via subscription but some articles are readable online.

SPECIAL FEATURES

Working along the top-of-page toolbar, **About ATG** explains the journal's focus and **News and Views** contains articles of topical interest, while **In Focus** examines a few items recently sold.

Fair and Auction Calendar presents the forthcoming couple of months, with dates highlighted in green, if an event is occurring. Auctions can also normally be viewed by location.

Internet Directory is a sizeable resource, well organised into categories which include Online Auctions, Auctioneers UK, Dealers UK and Useful Sites among many others, all of which load rapidly.

Eminently clear and rapid in construction, this website certainly deserves a visit from anyone seriously interested in antiques, not only those in the trade.

So exemplary is this website that the magazine, The World of Antiques & Art, earns its place here notwithstanding its Australian provenance.

SPECIAL FEATURES

Online Gallery, is located in the menu to the left-hand side of the page and leads to a search facility that can be used by item, dealer or category. **Current Issue** leads to an index of articles, though only those in highlighted print can be accessed online. As an example, under the title 'Mrs Chisholm's Federation Dress' there is currently a wonderfully lively article by Ian Hoskins about the celebrations that greeted Federation Day in Sydney a hundred years ago, with illustrations of the said dress, specially made for the occasion. **Articles** and **Back Issues** are self-explanatory links. **What's On** had no events listed in the UK on the occasion tested and would, in any case, be expected to have a mainly Australian bias.

Directory lists advertisers in the magazine, so the list of those in the UK is naturally somewhat limited. **Other Titles** offers onward links to the four other publications that WA produce, Collectables Trader, Antiques & Art in Queensland, Antiques in NSW and Antiques & Art in Victoria.

Well organised and simply presented, this is the website of a very attractive magazine.

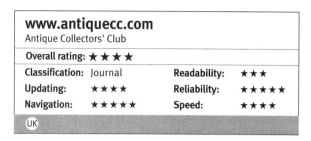

www.antiquecc.com
Antique Collectors' Club

Overall rating: ★ ★ ★ ★		
Classification: Journal	Readability:	★ ★ ★
Updating: ★ ★ ★ ★	Reliability:	★ ★ ★ ★ ★
Navigation: ★ ★ ★ ★ ★	Speed:	★ ★ ★ ★

UK

Formed in 1966, the club claims now to have a five figure, worldwide membership. They direct their operation deliberately at collectors in the middle and lower price-range rather than at the unattainable, museum-only level.

SPECIAL FEATURES

Who We Are introduces the club and explains its origins. **Our Publishers** lists the many fine and decorative arts publishers whose books they distribute, and which can be ordered online. **Request Catalog** allows you to fill in an online form (also to be found under New Book Mailing List). The remainder of the menu is a detailed list of collecting categories, under which you will find relevant books for sale.

Clicking on **Books**, in yellow on the centre of the homepage, only leads to another form, though this also offers a search facility, of limited sophistication. **Magazine** leads to details of 'Antique Collecting', the Club Journal, from which many past articles are readable online. The magazine can be ordered online.

This is one of those websites that seems quite limited in scope and then suddenly reveals hidden depths. The list of available books is impressive and specialised, while the magazine section of the site is thoroughly useful.

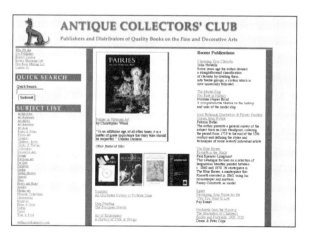

www.antiquesnews.co.uk
Antiques & Art Independent

Overall rating: ★ ★ ★ ★			
Classification:	Journal	**Readability:**	★ ★ ★ ★ ★
Updating:	Regular	**Reliability:**	★ ★ ★ ★
Navigation:	★ ★ ★ ★	**Speed:**	★ ★ ★ ★ ★

(UK) (US)

Subtitled 'The Newspaper for the British Antiques & Art Trade', this trade journal is still of real interest to private collectors. It is associated with the New England Antiques Journal, published in Massachusetts.

SPECIAL FEATURES

You can 'read' the online version of the paper simply by clicking either on the individual articles headlined on the homepage or on the successive page numbers at the bottom of the page. Pages, including illustrations, load quickly and the articles are snappily well written. For the printed version, which is more extensive and is the most widely circulated publication of its kind, you need to subscribe. There are five issues a year, with the UK annual subscription currently £13. It is only the relatively limited amount of information that can be gained from the internet version of the paper, as opposed to the hard-copy version, that produces a four-star rather than five-star overall rating above.

Simple and straightforward, this website is a useful shortcut method of keeping up with news in the antiques world, especially forthcoming events nationwide.

www.antiquesmagazine.com
Antiques Magazine

Overall rating: ★ ★ ★ ★			
Classification:	Journal	**Readability**	★ ★ ★
Updating:	Regular	**Reliability:**	★ ★ ★ ★
Navigation:	★ ★ ★ ★	**Speed:**	★ ★ ★ ★

(UK) (R) (£)

Antiques Magazine is only fully available to subscribers. A UK subscription online currently costs £52.00 (for 46 weekly issues), a major saving off the cover price as sold in the shops.

Click on 'enter' rather than 'welcome' to access the site. Sample contents are then seen by clicking on the items in the left-of-page index.

SPECIAL FEATURES

Bookshop is well-organised but of limited value so far. **TV and Radio**, however, is a very convenient short cut to finding out about forthcoming programmes of possible interest to collectors. The **Puzzle Page** presents a brief quiz and lets you 'estimate the estimate'. Answers are available immediately.

Weekly Features allows reading of articles in the current issue of the magazine. The **Auction and Fairs Calendars** are excellently detailed and load very rapidly.

The last three items in the homepage index are restricted to subscribers, namely **Art Prices Index, Antique Price Index** and **Articles Archive**. At the time of writing **Links** produced only one result, to Antiques Bulletin Online (see p.19).

If you have a broad-based rather than narrowly specialist interest in antiques, you could certainly do worse than subscribe to this magazine.

www.thisiscollecting.com

This is Collecting

Overall rating: ★ ★ ★ ★			
Classification: News service		**Readability:**	★ ★ ★ ★
Updating:	★ ★ ★ ★	**Reliability:**	★ ★ ★ ★
Navigation:	★ ★ ★	**Speed:**	★ ★ ★ ★

(UK)

This is a special news service from World Collectors' Net, and is a good way of keeping in touch with events in the collecting world: from auctions to articles about recent discoveries, such as items salvaged from shipwrecks.

SPECIAL FEATURES

Moving forward from the homepage involves clicking on one of the picture boxes, such as **Collecting News**, **Features**, **Auctions** or **Lorne's Diary**. This last recently carried a long and amusing article about the frustrations of a visit Lorne made to the Millennium Dome in the hope of discovering some really desirable collectables. Moving to any of the above pages produces a brief list down the left-hand margin, which may be an easier way of exploring the site as a whole. **Auctions**, at the time of writing, was headed by a forthcoming sale of James Bond memorabilia at Christie's - its most desirable item being Ursula Andress's bikini as worn in Dr No!

Be warned that the commercial logos on the right of the homepage will transport you to those websites and away from This is Collecting.

As a news service to keep you in touch with what's going on in the auctions world, this is useful.

Artefact

www.artefact.co.uk

The homepage introduces two magazines, Galleries, which focuses on fine art rather than antiques or collectables, and The Collector. This latter, first published in 1987, should not be confused with 'Collector' magazine (see p.29). The Collector is one of the better magazines for those seriously interested in antiques (rather than collectables), so it is a pity its online presence here is not more enticing. A short index includes antique dealers by name or location, but the slant is on those based in the south of the UK. Antiques Trade Support Services contained, at the time of writing, only three entries; one photographer, one carrier/shipper and one organiser of tours. Antiques Fairs offers a good list, with an associated key to Antiques Fair Organisers.

Collect it! Magazine

www.collectit.co.uk

Although Collect it! magazine is already, after three years, a firmly established favourite on the bookstalls, it has only recently adopted an internet presence and there is still a lot to do. The claim is that this will soon be the most comprehensive collecting site on the web. It will contain a Beginners' Guide to Collecting and the largest A-Z index of collecting topics anywhere. There will also be an online newsletter which will be emailed free to subscribers. The website is all a matter of promises at present, with little that any visitor can actually discover - though you can, of course, spend some money if you're really determined, buying one of half a dozen 'exclusive limited editions.'

Chapter 03
fairs and events

This could have been a very large section in the Guide, listing some of the multitude of smaller, local Fairs and Events organisers throughout the country. In fact, it contains only three websites. Adams and Penman Fairs are among the largest and best-known, so they warranted inclusion here; meanwhile the British Antique Dealers' Association website, though much more general in scope, does promote the BADA Fairs as its main feature. The gateway websites that fill the first section of this Guide, or the Journals in the second section, will be your route to finding out about smaller local events or specialist fairs.

www.adams-antiques-fairs.co.uk
Adams Antiques Fairs

Overall rating: ★ ★ ★ ★			
Classification:	Events	Readability:	★ ★ ★ ★
Updating:	★ ★ ★ ★ ★	Reliability:	★ ★ ★ ★
Navigation:	★ ★ ★ ★	Speed:	★ ★ ★ ★
UK			

Billing themselves as 'the longest running regular Sunday fairs in central London...', Adams run regular antiques and collectables fairs at the Royal Horticultural Hall (over 200 exhibitors), Chelsea Town Hall (80 exhibitors) and the Brocante Fair, which has in the past been held at Kensington Town Hall. This last is now moving to join the Vive la France Fair at Olympia. Another new venue for Adams in 2001 is Newbury Racecourse. The various venues are listed down the left-hand side of the homepage, each leading to further details of dates of forthcoming fairs being held there.

SPECIAL FEATURES

Information is admirably up to date; pictures load reasonably quickly and enough basic information is given to let you know whether a visit might be worth your while. The **Vive la France** events, held at Olympia, are dedicated to goods and services illustrating the typically French lifestyle; everything from food and wine to interior decoration and holidays (not especially antiques apart from the second-hand decorative goods that normally make up the **Brocante** events).

This website is practical and efficient rather than especially attractive. It would do enough, though, to tell you whether a visit would be worthwhile. As is often the case with fairs, most items for sale are relatively small and portable – a good hunting ground for gifts, of course.

www.penman-fairs.co.uk
Penman Fairs

Overall rating: ★ ★ ★ ★			
Classification:	Events	Readability:	★ ★ ★ ★
Updating:	Regular	Reliability:	★ ★ ★ ★ ★
Navigation:	★ ★ ★ ★	Speed:	★ ★ ★ ★
UK			

Caroline Penman launched the well-respected Penman Fairs over thirty years ago, using a continuous vetting procedure to ensure high standards.

SPECIAL FEATURES

Antiques Fairs leads to a list of forthcoming Penman Fairs in date order, with links to the individual events. Art Fairs does the same but leads to a much shorter list. **What's New**, at the time tested, only asked for suggestions about where to hold future fairs. **Links and Contact** tells you a bit more about the organisers, while **Exhibiting Dealers** lists all those who regularly take part, listed alphabetically with brief details of their specialisms and telephone contact details.

Complimentary Tickets enables you to print off your own tickets for two people or, if you don't have a printer, order them online.

A straightforward, easily used website of a practical rather than particularly informative nature.

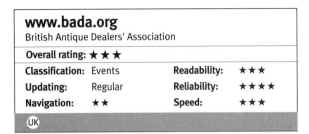

www.bada.org
British Antique Dealers' Association

Overall rating: ★ ★ ★			
Classification:	Events	**Readability:**	★ ★ ★
Updating:	Regular	**Reliability:**	★ ★ ★ ★
Navigation:	★ ★	**Speed:**	★ ★ ★

UK

Under the motto, 'Ars non habet inimicum nisi ignorantiam' (Art has no enemy but ignorance) and the medallion portrait of Benvenuto Cellini, we learn that BADA, the leading representative body for the antiques trade in the UK, was founded way back in 1918. (By the way, a mistake in entering the URL, using '.co.uk' rather than '.org', will take you to the British Audio Dealers' Association).

SPECIAL FEATURES

Members introduces BADA dealers in several different ways, sorted either alphabetically, or by location or by specialism. The overlapping of the indexing system leads to some confusion. If, for instance, you decide to search by specialism, say jewellery, and then select one business from the list (which admittedly appears very promptly), you find that your chosen business refuses to come up singly. Instead, a lengthy locality list is presented, with the names of the principal towns from which to select the right one. If you happen not to have noted the town where your chosen dealer was located you now have to use the 'back' button to check. And even then, when you identify the right town, you now obtain the list of all the dealers in that town, so you have to scroll through until you find the one specialising in jewellery. There should be a simpler method of getting at this information.

BADA takes you to a photograph of current chairman, the Rt Hon Peter Brooke, and to a list of other officers such as council members and regional representatives. Much more useful is **BADA Fairs**, which turns out to be the core of the website, offering details of the BADA Antiques and Fine Art Fair and lists of exhibitors, mostly with live onward links. It turns out that the event was voted Fair of the Year in 2000, so the 2001 Fair, (see under Events) has a high standard to maintain.

This is more a showcase for BADA's annual Fair than a website to visit for information about specific antiques or collecting interests. It is smart in appearance, certainly, but navigation could be improved.

Chapter 04

auctioneers

Auctioneers fall very clearly into two distinct types. First come the 'Big Four': Sotheby's, Christie's, Bonhams & Brooks, and Phillips, usually mentioned in that order, presumably because that is the order in which they were founded, and therefore presented in that order here.

Quite different are the online auctioneers, those who conduct auctions over the internet, not handling or seeing the items being sold at all. Of these the best known are Ebay, Ebid and QXL. Typically these auctioneers sell smaller, less 'antique' (in terms of age) items. They are all featured here, along with a few others perhaps less well known. This section then ends with the website of the Art Sales Index, the largest and most accurate online database of auction results throughout the world.

Having made it all sound very simple, of course, it now needs to be understood that the distinction is actually rather less cut and dried. Sotheby's, for example, conducts online auctions as well as real-world auctions, selling somewhat less valuable items by the former method. Meanwhile some of the online auctioneers offer articles on specialist collecting topics by experts, as well as links to dealers selling goods at fixed prices.

www.sothebys.co.uk and www.sothebys.com
Sotheby's

Overall rating: ★ ★ ★ ★			
Classification:	Auctions	Readability:	★ ★ ★ ★
Updating:	Regular	Reliability:	★ ★ ★ ★
Navigation:	★ ★ ★	Speed:	★ ★ ★ ★

US UK R

The famous, though recently somewhat turbulent auction house, founded in 1744 as a London book dealer, has its online presence here, with the UK and USA versions of the website being the same. Though no doubt having obvious attractions from the website management point of view, this proves slightly frustrating, as there appears to be no method of restricting your quest to Sotheby's operations in the UK alone. This might not matter, except that the amount of information here is so huge.

The search box that heads the homepage is immediately inviting and, if you know exactly what you are looking for, is a simple way to enter the website. Its efficiency is impressive, instantly producing, for example, 200 matches for the word 'Belleek', all linking to entirely relevant items in a number of different sales. As a first-time visitor, however, you may find using the blue tabs at the top of the page, an easier way in. Clicking on any one tab produces a set of sub-links in the grey bar immediately below.

SPECIAL FEATURES

The first important thing to realise is that **Auctions Online** and **Auction House** are separate, not covering the same ground. Bidding requires registration first.

Sotheby's Connoisseur offers a number of articles about specialist topics by Sotheby's experts. **Calendar** lists both exhibitions and forthcoming sales, with onward links (always underlined) that take you to further details of such events, often with online catalogues available for reading, and thumbnail illustrations where clicking produces an enlarged image. **Shop Sotheby's** takes you to publications, either Sotheby's own catalogues past and present, or a bookshop specialising in titles (some 'hard to find') about art and antiques. **Sotheby's Services** includes such items as **Financial Services** (where, among other things, you can arrange to borrow against the value of your collection, the minimum borrowing – yes, minimum – being half a million pounds!) and **Restoration**, leading to details of Sotheby's own in-house restorers.

About Sotheby's offers, under Corporate Information, a short review of Sotheby's history. While it may skate over the recent troubles of the firm, it still makes very interesting reading.

Site Search, the last of the tabs, produces a grey box at the bottom of the page, where you can find lists of Sotheby's Associates (more than 4,500 dealers) and Auction Results (prices achieved at recent sales), for which you need exact details of sale and lot numbers. This last is also available from the Auction House link.

From probably the most famous auction house in the world you would expect a detailed, well ordered website – and you get it. It's quite hard work to use, partly due to the density of information and partly to the small print, but it's top-grade stuff so worth the effort.

www.christies.com
Christie's

Overall rating: ★ ★ ★ ★			
Classification: Auctions		**Readability:**	★ ★ ★
Updating: ★ ★ ★ ★ ★		**Reliability:**	★ ★ ★ ★
Navigation: ★ ★ ★		**Speed:**	★ ★ ★ ★

UK

Sotheby's arch-rival has its website here, rich in highly informative detail but less than easy to explore.

The four-column homepage is not immediately easy to navigate. What look like links, in brown highlighted text, prove not to lead anywhere, whereas clicking on the pictures or the un-highlighted grey text produces results. Similarly, the bottom-of-page tabs do not in themselves lead to other pages. You only reach other areas of the website if you click on one of the drop-down options below the tabs, and very accurate mouse-work is needed not to slip into the list below an adjacent tab. Moreover, while fair-sized areas of white space are normally to be welcomed as a feature of website design, they are here so large as to make the text on many pages smaller (on a standard 14-inch monitor) than makes for comfortable reading.

SPECIAL FEATURES

The bottom-of-page tabs include **About Christie's**, offering Careers, Christie's History, How to Buy, How to Sell and Locations. **Sale Information** gives calendars of forthcoming auctions, results of past auctions, consignments (dates by which entries for forthcoming sales must be notified), press releases, Christie's Review and Webcasts (in January 2001 this page said 'No webcasts are scheduled until the New Year'). **Sale Categories**, ranging from Antiquities and Asian Art to Photographs & Prints, Wine & Cigars, is self explanatory; as is **Services**, under which are listed such topics as Estates & Appraisals, Books & Publications, Secure Storage and Christie's Education.

Services offers a Site Map, which duplicates the subject headings in the drop-down tabs. In fact, of course, there is a vast amount more information than the tabs indicate. As an example, exploration of the Department headed Furniture and Decorative Arts offers a long list of sub-headings, among them European Furniture and Decorative Objects. Further exploration reveals a link to Auction Records, a most interesting feature illustrating items that have fetched record prices, including several individual pieces of furniture that sold for over two million dollars, though from dates as far back as 1991 and 1993 when prices (before the crash of the Asian economies) were extremely high. As an indication of the movements in prices in recent years, such a feature could be most useful. A more detailed site-map, more like the index in an old-fashioned book, would help. Otherwise your chances of finding such a feature are down to either extremely assiduous trawling or mere serendipity. You will find a more general overview of saleroom records,

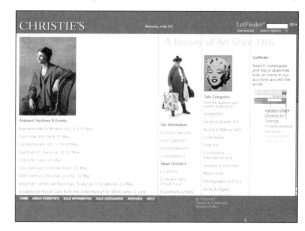

incidentally, under About Christie's, if you select History and then Exceptional Prices.

Sale prices given in dollars reveal a distinct American slant to this website, further confirmed by such spellings throughout the website as 'collectibles', 'colorful', 'fueled' and 'jewelry.' In a field where the historic 'Englishness' of Christie's might be assumed to be part of its cachet, this seems a little surprising. The strength of the American connection is also illustrated by the fact that the vast majority of Christie's Great Estates (see under Services) are examples of 'real estate' in North America. On the plus side, all the many pictures that appear throughout the website load with exemplary speed and clarity.

One part of the website that might become extremely useful is found under Services, headed **Christie's Images**. Here, a fully searchable database of images was advertised for Summer 2000. It is not, in fact, available yet. Well down the page is the opportunity to register online to be notified when it does eventually go live. Current information from this service, however, indicates that only some of the images will be viewable online by 'visitors' to the website. If you wish to see other images from the directory you will have to employ a Christie's Images researcher.

There is plenty of information here and many things to applaud, but getting at them is not as easy as it should be.

www.bonhams.com
Bonhams & Brooks

Overall rating: ★ ★ ★			
Classification:	Auctions	Readability:	★ ★ ★
Updating:	Regular	Reliability:	★ ★ ★ ★
Navigation:	★ ★ ★	Speed:	★ ★ ★

UK

At the time of writing, the merger between the well-known auction house, Bonhams, and the probably less-known (and much younger) Brooks was under way. The two websites were working independently, though both were accessible from this homepage. Whether this will remain the case is not known. The merged business will be the world's fourth largest auction house.

It's a smart-looking website where pages load quickly and most instructions are easy to follow. Pictures are slower to load, and a curious feature is that some links are not made apparent in the normal way, for example by colour, underlining or evident buttons. Some apparent links, where text appears in a different colour, turn out not to be operational. You can test the links by moving the cursor around until arrows appear, indicating where the links are.

SPECIAL FEATURES

The menu for Bonhams' website is in the left-hand margin. For a good introduction to the site, click on **Getting Started**. Access to the bidding areas of the site, as well as sale tracking and checking prices realised at auction, is only available to those who have signed in – for which purposes use Register for the first occasion and Sign In subsequently.

Catalogue Search offers two searching methods, by sale or by item, both clearly explained. **Auction Schedule** lists forthcoming sales, under such headings as Affordable Jewellery, Dogs in Art, and Valentine Sale. Further details of any sale are found by clicking on the sale number, to the left of the list, not on the location, which only leads to an address. Clicking on the picture alongside a catalogue entry will enlarge it for better viewing. The habit of using a picture of Bonhams' front door alongside those entries for which an illustration is, presumably, not available, is somewhat irritating. The policy of always presenting the main index down the left-hand side of every page, however, is helpful.

The remainder of the index is practical, addressing such matters as **Terms & Conditions, Insurance & Probate**, and **How to Find Us**. Probably more rewarding for the casual browser is Specialist Departments, which is divided into specialist categories, with interesting information about highlights of recent sales. Very unusually, no areas of the website are viewable offline, even those pages already opened.

The Brooks website is clearer, with the menu divided into six headings, **Sale Calendar, Catalogues, Subscriptions, Press Releases, Offices** and **Links**. Sales in this only ten-year-old company focus on such things as Sporting Memorabilia, Motor Cars and Automobilia, and Toys and Models, and the calendar starts with past sales, giving results, working forward to present and future sales. Catalogues, not readable online, can be ordered by email. Press Releases highlights results at recent sales. Links proves disappointing, currently leading only to Goodwood House, where some of Brooks' largest sales take place, and to Aon Corporation, insurance brokers.

Improvements could be made here, particularly to the usability of the site. The quality of the items for sale, however, is good without being too far out of reach of the ordinary collector, making the website worth investigating.

www.phillips-auctions.com
Phillips Auctioneers

Overall rating: ★ ★ ★ ★ ★			
Classification:	Auctions	**Readability:**	★ ★ ★ ★ ★
Updating:	Regularly	**Reliability:**	★ ★ ★ ★ ★
Navigation:	★ ★ ★ ★	**Speed:**	★ ★ ★ ★

UK

Harry Phillips set up this famous auction house in 1796 and, we are told, conducted sales of collections which belonged to Queen Marie-Antoinette, Beau Brummel and Napoleon among others. Today in the UK alone Phillips conducts over 800 sales a year.

SPECIAL FEATURES

This is an extensive website in which you will probably wish to start by clicking on London & UK, as opposed to the other options in rather faint print on the homepage, namely New York & USA, Sydney and Zurich. The London page now loads against a sophisticated brown background. The left-of-page index offers some basic history in **Welcome to Phillips**, and then **Auction Catalogues**, a list of forthcoming Phillips sales worldwide.

Buying & Selling briefly explains the bidding process, which can be conducted by fax, and then, under the headings Discovering What's On, Buying at Phillips and Selling at Phillips, such items as 'Obtaining a Sale Catalogue', 'Bidding if You Are Unable to Attend' and the reassuringly titled 'In the Unlikely Event that your Goods Don't Sell.'

Auction Calendar lists forthcoming auctions by category, starting with Aircraft and ending with Writing Equipment, via such other enticements as Mechanical Music, Postcards and Cigarette Cards, and – unique to Phillips as far as I know –

Scripophily & Bank Notes. Selling fine wines is another important feature of Phillips sales, mainly though not exclusively conducted in the USA.

The next few items in the main index are purely practical, such as how to subscribe to receive catalogues and how to contact Phillips around the world by various methods, including email. Buried among these, however, is **Phillips News**, which has a few well chosen items of news at any given time, usually with illustrations of special objects either on display in exhibitions or coming up for sale.

To interrogate **Sales Results** you need to know exact details of both sale and lot numbers. **Valuations On-line** is not quite what may be implied, as valuations are in fact normally conducted in person, verbal valuations being free and written ones charged. Here Phillips also offers its Inventory Management System, which consists of valuations delivered on CD using both text and images, a handy way of managing large collections. **Trusts and Estates Departments** is aimed mainly at those, such as the executors of wills, who may have large amounts of property to value and dispose of, or to list and protect.

Finally **Phillips-Selkirk** transports you to the plum-coloured North American part of the website, where the wine auctions are a special feature. In all other respects the information available duplicates that in the London & UK section, and a similar pattern fits Sydney (unexpectedly on almost the same background as the USA) and Zurich (green) also.

This stylish website is your route to finding out exactly where and when Phillips is auctioning fine art, antiques and wine around the world.

www.ebay.co.uk
Ebay

Overall rating: ★ ★ ★ ★			
Classification:	Online buy/sell	Readability:	★ ★ ★ ★ ★
Updating:	Regular	Reliability:	★ ★ ★
Navigation:	★ ★ ★ ★ ★	Speed:	★ ★ ★ ★ ★

UK R

Britain's best known and largest (in terms of numbers of items for sale) auction site. Note that there is an American twin website at www.ebay.com. Explore that as well, but remember that there would be shipping and possible Customs costs, should you order anything. This is an 'online trading community' in which items are sold person-to-person, not via an auction house as such. There is automatic insurance cover for buyers on items up to £120 in value and there is now an online dispute resolution service hosted by Square Trade, but you are still dependent on the honesty of the participants, hence the modest reliability score above.

SPECIAL FEATURES

Anyone can browse this website but actual buying or selling requires registration, which is free. It involves keying in your name and contact details, waiting for an email acknowledgment from Ebay (normally within 24 hours) and being issued with a User ID. At the time of writing, the newsdesk on the Antiquesweb site (see p.21) was reporting a real threat to Ebay's future, in the shape of a multiple lawsuit being brought against the company in California.

To explore the website, which is very large indeed, go first to Antiques & Art and then select from a list of categories. The number of current items for sale in each category is indicated by a figure in brackets in the index. You will probably need a quick visit to **Help** and then **Glossary of**

Terms in order to understand the little picture-logos that accompany some items, if not the terms themselves. Near the top of any category page you can reduce the list of items in one of three ways, by moving from Current (the complete list, which comes up automatically) to New Today, Ending Today or Going, Going, Gone.

Some categories, such as Ceramics, may contain very large numbers of items. In this case it is worth using the search box at the top of the page, entering a specific make such as 'Masons', ticking 'search only Art & Antiques: Ceramics' and seeing if you get a helpful result. On the occasion tested, this reduced a list of over four hundred items to only five, which was clearly a considerable time-saver.

Once you reach the page of an item you are interested in, there is a lot of information available, such as the current state of bidding and the amount of time left. The Description box at the top left of any such page leads to more details of the item itself and, nearly always, a picture. Underneath the name of the seller are various options, including 'view comments in seller's Feedback Profile', which is a useful way of checking how reliable the seller may be. To the right of any item's page you will find two other options whereby you can pass on details to a friend, or keep the bidding progress of the item in view until nearer the end of the auction period.

The bidding process is explained under **Help**, and this is also the place to look for answers to 'Top Questions'. **Community** is where the website goes interactive and is also where the Library is located. This good place to look for a brief article on any particular collecting topic. You will find that this part of the website is more US-based than UK-based, with nearly all topic-specific events being in North America, but that doesn't stop the articles being of relevance.

For person-to-person buying and selling this is undoubtedly the most active UK website, with a good record of reliability.

www.ebid.co.uk
eBid Auctions

Overall rating: ★ ★ ★ ★

Classification:	Online auctions	**Readability:**	★ ★ ★ ★ ★
Updating:	Regular	**Reliability:**	★ ★ ★
Navigation:	★ ★ ★ ★	**Speed:**	★ ★ ★ ★ ★

UK R

There is, of course, an American partner site, found at www.ebid.com, but UK users will probably want to start here to explore what will normally be a short list of antiques (a couple of dozen only, perhaps) for sale and a very much longer list of collectables.

You need to register to take part fully in this website (a very simple matter, producing a password in your email 'within a few minutes') but there is nothing to stop you exploring it first. The website sells everything, but four categories may be of interest to the readers of this book, namely Antiques, Beanie Babies, Books & Magazines and Collectibles. The last of these may contain several thousand items, though the majority are likely to be postage stamps.

SPECIAL FEATURES

Clicking on any of the four categories above will lead to a further list of sub-categories that, in the case of **Collectibles** for instance, includes Fine Art, Autographs, Die-cast toys of various sorts, Music (probably the second largest category), Orientalia, Railwaylia (sic), Science Fiction and so on. Note that you may have to scroll down the page to below the list of Featured Auctions to find these. Many items are looking for bids in the tens of pounds range but every now and then you come across something for which a large sum is being sought, such as £4,495 for 'an England 2006 poster'.

Curiosity getting the better of you, you click for further details and learn that this is apparently one of only fifteen posters made for England's bid to host the football World Cup in that year, a bid now rejected. One day, it might indeed be worth a lot of money!

In the case of **Beanie Babies**, most items will, of course, be in the 'Retired' and 'Rare' categories, with Nipponia the Japanese Bear apparently being particularly desirable.

Clicking on **Make a Bid** on the homepage leads to a helpdesk list of instructions. Rather oddly, this list starts with the question 'How do I find out how my auction ended?' but perhaps that is because this is the most frequently asked question. Just above the top of the list are half a dozen links, including myebid (an explanation of the bid-tracking system), after the auction and money (how to pay).

The third homepage option is **Sell an Item**, which again leads to a list of easily understood instructions and gives details of any charges you will incur. Finally, at the foot of the homepage you will find several other links in brackets, including **Soap Box**, which is eBid's discussion forum. **Escrow** (eBid claims a first in offering this service) and **Insurance** lead to some of the safeguard facilities offered by this website, for instance the system whereby you can pay your money to a third party, only actually paying once the purchased item has been released.

User-friendly and manageable, it is no wonder this is one of the busiest auction sites on the web.

www.icollector.com
icollector – iseek.ifind.ideal

Overall rating: ★ ★ ★ ★ ★			
Classification:	Auctions	**Readability:**	★ ★ ★ ★ ★
Updating:	Regular	**Reliability:**	★ ★ ★ ★
Navigation:	★ ★ ★ ★	**Speed:**	★ ★ ★ ★ ★

UK R

This is a large but uncomplicated website, calling itself 'the independent connection to the world's auction houses' and, founded in 1994, claiming to be the first site of its kind. A box at the top right of the homepage gives the figures for the number of items, and auction houses represented on the site each day.

The coloured buttons along the top of the page lead to Auction House Sales, Dealers & Galleries, Online Auctions, Library and Channels. If you want to buy and sell online, you'll need to submit your details, via the Register link. At Auction House Sales you can choose to view events either by the name of the auction house or by category of sale. The complete list is viewed by scrolling down the page and each sale links to a page giving further details. If absentee bidding is possible it is made evident under the auction house name.

SPECIAL FEATURES

Dealers & Galleries offers the opportunity to buy works of art, antiques or collectables at fixed prices, from businesses worldwide. **Online Auctions** is what you would expect, though the number of items for sale is relatively small. **Library** contains a short list of articles by experts.

This delivers everything to be expected of a gateway website, acting as an umbrella for a worldwide range of salerooms and dealers.

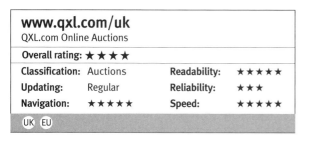

www.qxl.com/uk
QXL.com Online Auctions

Overall rating: ★ ★ ★ ★			
Classification:	Auctions	Readability:	★ ★ ★ ★ ★
Updating:	Regular	Reliability:	★ ★ ★
Navigation:	★ ★ ★ ★ ★	Speed:	★ ★ ★ ★ ★

UK EU

This well-known auctioneering website sells everything under the sun, just as Ebay does, and the homepage similarly offers links that narrow the field a bit, two of which are Antiques and Collectables. It conducts person-to-person and business-to-person auctions throughout western Europe.

SPECIAL FEATURES

New to QXL? is a good place to start exploring this extensive website. The same page offers **How to Bid** and **How to Sell** buttons, which give a basic outline of the process. It is necessary to register to participate fully. Much of the site can still be explored without registering, however.

Clicking on **Browse** and then on Antiques leads to a well-organised page in which the various collecting categories and sub-categories are intelligently grouped – though quite why Scientific Instruments should come under Clocks & Watches, rather than the other way round, is not clear. The number of items currently for sale in each category is indicated in brackets, with Antique Jewellery, Books & Manuscripts and Fine Art typically being the largest. Click to select a collecting topic from the list and you will then be offered brief details of all relevant items, with the key to picture-logos helpfully given on each page, and the date and time at which the auction ends. Clicking on an individual item brings up further details, usually with a picture. There

are some surprises, for instance a selection of six Japanese maples (yes, live trees) listed under Japanese Works of Art, alongside four ivory netsuke – but coming across the unexpected is part of what makes this game interesting.

Collectables (accessed via Browse on the homepage) produces a much longer list of categories, several containing more than 1,000 items and Comics typically more than 10,000! The process thereafter, however, is the same.

Note that the widely advertised connection with Hugh Scully is available from two picture boxes on the right of the Antiques section main page. One of these is to his valuation service, which is well explained and currently costs £7.50 per item to be assessed. A valuation is emailed back to you.

QXL deserves its flagship reputation, with a detailed, user-friendly website and a reputation for fair dealing.

www.theauctionchannel.com
The Auction Channel

Overall rating: ★ ★ ★ ★

Classification:	Auctions	Readability:	★ ★ ★ ★
Updating:	★ ★ ★	Reliability:	★ ★ ★ ★
Navigation:	★ ★ ★	Speed:	★ ★ ★ ★

UK US

The Auction Channel transmitted its first live auction, 'Beatles for Sale', with Bonhams in March 1997. By the end of that year it had launched its Interactive Bidding System (IBS) and NetBidLive was introduced in December 1998. Now owned, since 1999, by Brilliant Digital Entertainment Inc. of Los Angeles, it enables live, online bidding at certain well-known auction houses all over the world by means of either the Internet or a touch-tone telephone. Participants can also view the progress of auctions on satellite or cable television.

SPECIAL FEATURES

Start with **About Us** in the top of the black header-bar for an explanation of how The Auction Channel differs from other auctioneering websites. The further explanations of how the live bidding process works are accessed from halfway down the left-of-page margin, under 'How do I make and absentee bid?' and 'How do I bid using NetBidLive?' in the New to the Auction Channel? box.

In mid-January 2001, The Auction Channel had neither any immediate nor any forthcoming auctions listed under **Today's Auctions** or **Upcoming Auctions**, which was disappointing. Much more rewarding was exploration of the material at the bottom of the homepage, relating to recently held sales.

Magazine is accessed from the header bar, and well worth visiting, with a wide selection of interesting articles, loosely divided under the headings Behind the Scenes, Around the Houses, The Expert (two important articles here explain the additional costs that face both buyers and sellers at auction, in terms of additional premiums, possible storage costs for items unsold and the like) and Post Sale Reports. A visit to **Community** indicates that the website is not yet being much used for online discussion, with many more questions being posed than answered, and the wine discussion area being almost empty.

This stylish and generally articulate website has potential, though it is not yet being used to anything like its full capability. Only time will tell whether greater success lies ahead but the approach is professional, which ensures the four-star rating.

www.fsauctions.co.uk
FSauctions

Overall rating: ★ ★ ★ ★			
Classification: Auctions		Readability:	★ ★ ★ ★
Updating:	★ ★ ★ ★	Reliability:	★ ★ ★
Navigation:	★ ★ ★ ★	Speed:	★ ★ ★

UK R

www.art-sales-index.com
Art Sales Index

Overall rating: ★ ★ ★ ★ ★			
Classification: Sales Index		Readability:	★ ★ ★ ★ ★
Updating:	Regular	Reliability:	★ ★ ★ ★ ★
Navigation:	★ ★ ★ ★ ★	Speed:	★ ★ ★ ★

UK R £

Hosted by Freeserve, FSauctions is one of the simpler auction websites to explore. You need to register, free of charge, to use the site and then wait for a unique password to be emailed to you before you can start buying and selling.

Double click on the text of the tabs across the top of the page to link through to different areas of the site.

SPECIAL FEATURES

Art & Antiques, Beanies and Collectibles are the three areas heading the menus to the left. Clicking on any of these leads to further menus. Ceramics & Porcelain, incidentally, will be found under Collectibles, whereas Kitchen, Dinner & Tableware and Vases & Decorative Bowls come under Antiques & Crafts, a somewhat arbitrary division.

Visit our Collectibles Arcade, a picture-box to the top right of the Collectibles page, introduces a few of the website's regular contributors, with brief details of the specialist areas in which they deal.

It is noticeable that on any given day, even where the end of the auction period is imminent, many items are attracting no bids at all. Though not too encouraging for sellers, this might, of course, make it a good place from which to buy!

The claim is a big one, namely that this is the most accurate database of fine art auction results in the world. Certainly, with over 2 million results going back over fifty years, it is impressive.

There is no access without payment, and the service is not cheap, so you would need to use it a lot to justify subscribing. Current rates are a subscription of £140 per year and then an hourly rate for use, timed to the second. You can, however, apply for a free trial. To do this, click on Database on the homepage and then on 'Click Here to register for a free trial', which will produce a simple form where the only field you are required to fill in is your email address. The response is rapid and gives you a week's free entry to the site, so this is well worth doing.

Once in, it is important first to read the instructions for how to search. Note that, unusually, pressing return will not activate the search, only clicking on the 'search' button. Where large numbers of works by a particular artist are listed, one of the quickest ways to refine the search is probably by defining the medium, for instance 'oil painting', but if only a few works are listed anyway, then simply click on 'display' at the bottom of the form (you may have to scroll down to see this button). As an alternative to time-limited free entry, a pay-as-you-go facility is being introduced.

SPECIAL FEATURES

For those who may need the service more than once but not all that often, click on **Enquiry Service** on the homepage. This allows you to make a request by post, telephone or email. The results are then sent to you, at a cost of £10 per page (15 entries).

Book Store contains principally those books published by Art Sales Index Ltd. All the books relate to prices in the art world, rather than a broader range. **CD Rom** offers the opportunity to buy details of auction sales results over recent years, divided by the decade. The 1990/2000 CD-rom is available from May 2001. Subscribing once, at a price of £350 plus VAT, entitles you to annual updates thereafter at a price of £115 plus VAT.

Graphs & Charts are available to all visitors to the website and are interesting in that they show very clearly that the peaks in prices achieved in the late 1980s are still far from being matched, over ten years on. Note that you will need to use your bottom-of-page scroll bar to view all the graphs.

Links is a particularly valuable part of the website, with a good list under Auction Houses, all with onward connections to the relevant websites, and an exceptional list under Magazines and Publishers, containing links to some of the best fine art magazines worldwide. Galleries at present produces only half a dozen links, though one of these is to Paintbox UK, which might be quite an interesting site to visit if you felt able to identify a possible star of the future, as the artists whose work is shown are all contemporary. Other Services & Sites is a somewhat eclectic list of websites, mainly of a practical service nature, worldwide.

This is a highly professional website offering a very valuable search facility and an excellent set of Links. It deserves exploration.

miscellaneous

This section could be conveniently sub-titled 'Importing, Exporting, Retrieving, Conserving'. It lists two web-pages giving Customs guidance about the import of antiques, one from LAPADA about export, two websites addressing the issue of theft and the recovery of stolen objects, and three about repair or conservation.

Do please note the presence here of the Invaluable website. Its main focus is the protection of your treasures from thieves, which is what has put it into this section, but it contains a great deal more besides and is an excellent resource, so you should not lose sight of it because it has ended up here rather than with the gateway websites at the beginning of this Guide.

www.excessbaggage.co.uk/customs/uk.asp
Customs Guide – United Kingdom

Overall rating: ★ ★ ★ ★ ★			
Classification: Customs		**Readability:**	★ ★ ★ ★ ★
Updating: Regular		**Reliability:**	★ ★ ★ ★ ★
Navigation: ★ ★ ★ ★		**Speed:**	★ ★ ★
UK			

This is the most straightforward and condensed of various sites advising about the regulations for moving antiques between countries.

SPECIAL FEATURES

Four columns are headed **Goods, Documents Required, Customs Prescriptions** and **Remarks**. Move well down the page to where the Goods column is headed 'Works of Art, Antiquities.' For Customs purposes, anything over 100 years old comes under this heading. The Remarks column explains that objects imported into the UK for resale are treated as commercial imports and are therefore dutiable and/or subject to VAT. Articles forming part of a household removal, or bought for personal use and certified as being over 100 years old, are not.

A good website for demystifying the question of what is, and is not, dutiable when imported from abroad. This is not detailed, however. For more information try HM Customs & Excise (see p.50).

www.findstolenart.com
Find Stolen Art

Overall rating: ★ ★ ★ ★ ★			
Classification: Stolen items		**Readability:**	★ ★ ★ ★ ★
Updating: ★ ★ ★ ★		**Reliability:**	★ ★ ★ ★ ★
Navigation: ★ ★ ★ ★ ★		**Speed:**	★ ★ ★ ★
UK			

This website exists to help police forces nationwide track down stolen goods, and to help dealers and collectors follow the due diligence code. It is not restricted to art works.

SPECIAL FEATURES

Navigation here is straightforward, with two major lists of items, under the headings **Stolen** and **Recovered**, divided into categories such as furniture, glass and jewellery. Each item is then listed separately, illustrated with a thumbnail picture, which may be enlarged by clicking. Some items are not illustrated and most are dependent on home snaps rather than professional photographs, of course, a fact that may remind collectors of the importance of taking good, clear pictures of any items of value. The numbers of items in any given category is a neat indicator of what thieves are most inclined to target – six pages of items under Furniture but nothing under Costume, Fans & Dolls or Musical Instruments, for example. It would help to know how long items remain in the database but this information was not immediately evident.

In the grey box on the homepage there is much interesting information to be found about theft of art and antiques under the headings **All Articles, In the Press** and **News**.

Of the various theft-tracing websites, this is one of the clearest and most readily usable.

www.thesaurus.co.uk

Invaluable (powered by Thesaurus)

Overall rating: ★ ★ ★ ★ ★			
Classification:	Stolen items	Readability:	★ ★ ★ ★ ★
Updating:	Daily	Reliability:	★ ★ ★ ★
Navigation:	★ ★ ★ ★ ★	Speed:	★ ★ ★ ★ ★

UK

Calling itself 'the leading collectors' portal on the Web', Invaluable certainly got in ahead of the game, as it was founded with the specific aim of applying IT solutions to the auction industry as far back as 1989. It offers two principal online facilities, to search auction catalogues and to help protect items in public and private collections. As an adjunct to the latter aim, it hosts an excellent service for featuring – and hoping to provoke the recovery of – stolen items.

SPECIAL FEATURES

A somewhat busy homepage immediately offers a keyword search facility, as well as **News** and **Feature**, both divided under the headings This Week, Last Week and Archive. Welcome introduces the Invaluable concept.

Stolen illustrates an uncomfortably long list of items stolen in recent weeks, mostly from private homes, with details of which police force to contact if you have any information to offer that might lead to their recovery. Among links on this page is Invaluable Protector, a service that will check auction houses around the world for your stolen items on a daily basis, as well as publicising the loss to police, dealers and collectors, and making use of the Invaluable Police Liaison Team, presided over by a former head of Scotland Yard's Art and Antiques Squad. Invaluable Tracer will use its databases to try and find your missing items and Invaluable Recoveries tells some success stories.

Invaluable Top Ten currently lists the theft from the Isabella Stewart Gardner Museum in Boston as the greatest art heist of all time, while Jan and Hubert van Eyck's painting 'The Just Judges', stolen from a church in Ghent, tops the individual list. The last of these links, **Stolen Art News**, makes very interesting reading. At the bottom of the same page, **Smarter Homes** leads to information about cutting-edge security devices; **Finder's Keepers?** might be expected to address the question of what one may or may not keep, but turns out for some reason to be about the Alfred Dunhill Museum collection of cigarette lighters, powder compacts and the like. Another current link is about Heritage Theft.

Finder introduces the various levels of service to which you can subscribe in pursuit of that elusive item. After that comes **Auctions**, which offers a calendar of the current month and invites you to consult a list for either the next seven or the next 14 days. Clicking on one of these options will then bring up a list in date order, ranging from the most well-known auction houses to some much smaller ones, and even some abroad. Clicking on the name in each instance brings up contact details, the time of both the sale and the prior viewing arrangements, the percentage buyer's premium, if known, and the approximate number of lots.

Appraiser is an online valuation service, aimed mostly at professionals, while **Chat** and **Forum** are what you would expect, the latter making interesting reading. **Links** goes to an excellent list of other websites, each with a brief description. One of these is the Antique Collectors Club, in association with Invaluable, which offers long lists of books on specialist collecting topics.

Given the number of photographs, this website is admirably rapid. More importantly, it performs a vital service and, above all, is genuinely interesting – so its name, Invaluable, just about sums it up.

www.ukic.org.uk
United Kingdom Institute for Conservation

Overall rating: ★ ★ ★ ★ ★			
Classification:	Conservation	**Readability:**	★ ★ ★ ★ ★
Updating:	Regular	**Reliability:**	★ ★ ★ ★ ★
Navigation:	★ ★ ★ ★	**Speed:**	★ ★ ★ ★ ★

UK

UKIC represents professional conservators and restorers nationwide, both working in private practice and in institutions such as museums and art galleries. Its role is to encourage both knowledge and skills in conservation through education and the exchange of information.

SPECIAL FEATURES

An **Introduction to UKIC** is probably the best place to start on your first visit to the site. **Professional Accreditation of Conservator Restorers** is aimed at practitioners but is no doubt of interest to anyone wishing to be assured about standards.

Publications introduces Conservation News, the three-issues-a-year newsletter of UKIC, Grapevine, the calendar of events (the only publication on this page to which there is a live link), and The Conservator, an annual journal of 'authoritative papers.' At the bottom of this page is a link headed **Full List of Publications For Sale** (the same as the homepage link entitled simply Publications), which leads to a fascinating list on topics such as Restoration of Early Musical Instruments, Lacquerwork and Japanning, The Analysis of Pigments and Plasters, and Dust, Dirt and Debris. These are not available for reading online, though an online ordering facility was in preparation at the time of writing.

Other links include **Conferences and Meetings** on the home page, which immediately leads to **Current Calendar**, listing events open to members. **Specialist Sections** is duplicated by the pictures on yellow bands in the margins of the homepage. **Membership** explains the various categories of membership available, with full membership costing just over £60 at the time of writing, and associate membership half that sum. **Members Area** is restricted only to those who have already joined.

Although aimed at professional conservators rather than the general public, there is much that is interesting here. Certainly a website that rewards exploration.

www.bafra

British Antique Furniture Restorers' Association

Overall rating: ★ ★ ★ ★			
Classification: Restoration		**Readability:**	★ ★ ★ ★ ★
Updating:	★ ★ ★	**Reliability:**	★ ★ ★ ★
Navigation:	★ ★ ★ ★ ★	**Speed:**	★ ★ ★ ★

(UK)

This organisation has nothing to sell but the skills of its members, whom this website introduces.

SPECIAL FEATURES

The links on the blue index panel are straightforward and clear. The first item, **Finding a Conservator-Restorer**, leads to a brief introductory article and then a list of counties in which restorers are located. As not all top-quality restorers necessarily choose to be members of Bafra, the list, which contains only Bafra members, is relatively short. Some counties, like Northumberland and Durham, for example, appear to contain no furniture restorers at all. Using a Bafra restorer, however, would give you certain safeguards. **Bafra Membership** explains the various levels of competence restorers have to display. **Further Information on Bafra** includes a history of the Association, founded in 1978.

Bafra News gives information about recent events, and currently features the results of the BAFRA/Martin Student Conservation Awards 2000. This is the only area of the website to have photographs, of the items restored by both the winner and the runner-up. **Forthcoming Events** was, in January 2001, still headed 'Events in 2000' and no onward link was available. **Articles on Restoration** contains five specialist articles, one of which is on The Air Improvement Centre and is effectively an advertisement for that organisation. The others are on specific restoration projects,

apart from a good general article by John Kitchen, retired head of furniture and woodwork conservation at the Victoria and Albert Museum.

Friends of Bafra introduces the benefits of becoming a Friend, which include access to special events and lectures by Association members. **Student Section** leads to Splinters, the group for trainee restorers, whether still at college or in early jobs. Finally there is a somewhat uneven list of other websites available under **Links to Other Sites**. This begins with English Heritage, UKIC (see p.48) and BADA (see p.32) and, mentioning a small number of museums all in London, ends with several websites of interest to those in the woodworking field.

This is a tidy, simply designed website that contains nothing to annoy – and nothing much to inspire either. It could do so much more.

www.conservationconsortium.com
Conservation Consortium

Overall rating: ★ ★ ★			
Classification:	Conservation	**Readability:**	★ ★ ★ ★
Updating:	Regular	**Reliability:**	★ ★ ★ ★
Navigation:	★ ★ ★ ★ ★	**Speed:**	★ ★ ★ ★

UK

This is a website compiled to put you in touch with specialist conservators or restorers throughout the UK.

SPECIAL FEATURES

If you click on the **Choosing a Conservator** link you are then offered a list down the left-hand side of the page from which to choose anything from Archaeology and Archives to Wall Painting and Wood. Selecting one of these will usually lead to sub-categories that enable you to specify more accurately what you are seeking to have conserved or restored. A quick survey of the businesses listed seems to suggest that the majority are in the south of England, but this is nevertheless an important resource.

Conservation or restoration of items in collections is of importance to all serious collectors and a website of this nature is therefore to be welcomed, especially if, over time, it proves to expand and list businesses further afield.

OTHER SITES OF INTEREST

Her Majesty's Customs & Excise: Imported Antiques, Notice 362

www.hmce.gov.uk/notices/362.htm
From the vast number of government leaflets about importing goods, this one, dating from April 1998, is the most relevant for those buying antiques. These pages explain in detail HM Customs regulations governing the import of antiques. Articles include such topics as 'Can I import antiques by post?' and 'What evidence of age can Customs accept?' as well as '702 Vat Imports' and '718 Margin schemes for second-hand goods, works of art, antiques and collectors' items'.

LAPADA – Exporting Art and Antiques

www.lapada.co.uk/services/expsvcs.html
The rules governing the export of antiques are considerably more elaborate than those for importing. This affects those antiques dealers and others who are selling to customers abroad, but also, of course, visitors buying antiques in the UK and wishing to take them home. The main page here is divided under four headings: VAT Advice for Visitors (which includes information about how to reclaim VAT on goods exported outside the EU), Packing and Shipping, Certificates of Age for Antiques, and Export Licences. The links in purple at the top of this page merely lead to the relevant paragraphs within it, not to additional material.

See also main Lapada review on p.17

collecting categories

This section of the Guide introduces a whole range of websites on specific collecting topics. These topics are listed alphabetically and, typically, each category is represented by one or two prime websites, followed by a number of further recommendations. Remember, though, that probably the most successful first port of call for any of these topics may still be the general gateway sites, such as Antiques UK (see p.12) or the BBC's Antiques website (see p.15). It is really important not to ignore these larger, more general portals, because in many cases they will still give you the best basic information of all. The following websites are therefore suggested in support of the gateway websites, not instead of them.

It is not possible to mention every conceivable collecting category. Please don't be disappointed if your own particular collecting interest does not appear in this list. The chances are that from a different, closely related topic you may be able to find a link to something of more use. As an example, if you are interested in scripophily (the collecting of banknotes) you will probably find material that will help you under headings like ephemera or coins.

Even after you have exhausted the possibilities mentioned here, you will probably still want to continue doing your own searches using a good search engine. For this purpose, my personal recommendation would unquestionably be Google (www.google.co.uk). The responses it brings you are more accurately targeted and more generously described than you are likely to find elsewhere.

Also, with Google there is the useful possibility of restricting your quest to UK-based websites. Select 'Pages from the UK' rather than 'The Web' (under the main search box). This may not be what you want to do on every occasion, and it is certainly not to imply that American or, indeed, websites of any other national origin are in any way inferior. But you need to be aware that American sites do at present outnumber British ones by miles and will probably continue to do so. As an example, the one and a half million 'hits' that a general web search produces in response to the word 'antiques' is immediately reduced to under forty thousand if you select the 'Pages from the UK' option. If you are looking for an informative museum collection to visit, or a dealer or auctioneer from whom to buy, then restricting your quest in this way may be very relevant.

As you become more experienced at searching, you will begin to recognise various gateway websites making regular appearances in response. For example, virtually every antiques collecting question you put will immediately be answered by at least one, if not several, responses from Ebay, the online auction site (see p.38). This is because someone will be trying to sell an item, or several items, which match the search 'object' you have specified. Clicking on that webpage to have a closer look will bring up details of the object(s) in question, but this is not what you are looking for if you are in pursuit of information about the collecting interest rather than merely seeking to buy.

In the same manner, any results in a search engine that start 'Amazon' will take you to a book or books, available to order from Amazon.com. Amazon is a wonderful facility; its searches are cleverly targeted, and books are often delivered very promptly indeed. An entire book to read on the subject, however, may not be what you want if you are looking for immediate information, readable online.

Similarly, results that start 'About...' or 'How to', or have 'about.com' as part of their URL, will almost certainly take you to the pages of About.com, a vast American directory, where the information you can dig out will have a definite American slant and will often not be very detailed. An example might be the response to your search enquiry 'coin collecting.' The response 'About Coin Collecting' would at first glance seem to be precisely what you are looking for. Click on it, however, and you will almost certainly find that the next page offers various articles about that subject but from the perspective of a US-based collector and therefore concentrating on US coins such as gold eagles and Lincoln pennies. Meanwhile, the meat of what you will be offered from any About.com pages is access to dealers, and they will almost always be located in the USA.

By contrast, another frequent response, when you input a collecting category into a search engine, will quite likely come from the Dmoz Open Directory Project. This may prove much more productive in terms of offering you the information you need, as Dmoz is a directory of information sources, not a selling operation. A typical Dmoz Open Directory page will be headed by the topic you have requested, say 'Antique Clocks', and then a number of websites divided under headings such as History, Repairs, Shopping and so on. To understand how this directory works and how it is assembled, visit www.dmoz/org/about.html, where the process of using volunteers to contribute is clearly explained – and the page ends with the encouraging words 'HUMANS do it better.' Within Dmoz, some of the topics or categories have yet to receive any input at all, so if you find an 'empty' page and feel you could contribute you may wish to click on the 'Become an Editor' button and start a list of links yourself.

Sometimes the search criteria need to be very specifically defined. For instance, a search for 'science objects' might benefit from being entered in a more advanced search facility. Using the Google model, you could open up 'Advanced Search' and then put those two words into the main box, combining it with the words 'vintage, period, antique, historic' in the second box, and excluding the term 'fiction' in the third. This would ensure that none of the results would offer you 'science fiction.' Even with the most specific of search requests, however, you can still come adrift, as I discovered when looking for good websites about collecting silver. The words 'silver' and 'collecting' produced (admittedly among many more relevant websites) one on collecting the lesser silver diving beetle – not quite what I had in mind!

When using a search engine such as Google, make use of as many different terms as possible – for instance, 'period', 'early', 'vintage' or 'historic' and even words like 'forgotten' and 'lost' may be just as useful as the word 'antique.' Any of these, placed in front of the item you are looking for, such as 'vintage corkscrews', for example, may produce results. Similarly, don't forget words that dealers and collectors themselves may use, such as 'bygones' and 'curios.'

Some websites have inconveniently small print, at least as it appears on a standard 14" screen. Sometimes, but not always, you can adjust this by going into 'View' and then 'fonts' and enlarging the point-size. Similarly a few websites allow you to change the colour of, for instance, the backgound to a page, which may be another way of making print easier to read. If these options are available the website itself will normally tell you.

Some websites will ask you to register or subscribe to gain access to all areas of the information they provide. Sometimes this merely involves giving your name, your email address and your choice of password, rather than actually paying any money. Giving your contact details may enable the website concerned to send you what they, no doubt, would call further useful information. You might call it unsolicited material. If you get caught in this way, don't worry. You should always be offered the option to un-subscribe if you wish.

Payments, whether as subscriptions to websites or in exchange for goods, are a matter of anxiety for many internet users. Website businesses and owners are increasingly aware of this and realise that if the internet is to flourish as a marketplace and become a respected part of the new economy it must offer very secure online dealing facilities. Some websites use a little padlock symbol to indicate special secure dealing arrangements; others have 'https' rather than merely 'http' as the letters that preface their URLs; others offer you information about security when you reach the stage of filling in online order forms. It is no more dangerous to give your credit card details in these circumstances than it is to use it to order goods by telephone or to allow it to be taken away from your table in a restaurant for payment.

While on the topic of payments, if you are surfing a lot and consequently spending a great deal of time connected to the internet, you will be conscious of the cost. There are various ways of managing this aspect of internet use. One is to subscribe to a telephone package that gives you a reduced-cost service at evenings and weekends, and then try to restrict your internet use to those times. It is very noticeable that the system can operate more slowly, however, at times when America is awake and online, so this may also be worth taking into account. You may alternatively be able to list your internet dial-up number as a 'best friend' number, on which you get a reduction.

Finally, if you think you really are going to become an antiques addict and a heavy user, you should consider subscribing to a one-off package, typically in the £100-per-year or £20-per-month bracket, that will give you unlimited online time twenty-four hours a day. Details of such services can be found by putting the words 'unmetered internet uk' into a search engine. Don't confuse this with 'free access', which probably only means you are not being charged for the initial connection to the internet provider, but are still paying for your online time. All sorts of options are offered, such as one week in three completely free from Strayduck (www.strayduck.co.uk).

I hope this has been helpful. Good luck.

arts & crafts, art nouveau, art deco

In recent years, the art and design of the late nineteenth and early twentieth centuries has become so fashionable as to be virtually a craze. Several magazine articles have featured people who have managed to furnish and decorate their homes completely in, say, Art Deco style. As a consequence you will find any number of online dealers and auctioneers offering goods from this period for sale. You will also find it something of a collecting minefield, as there are many fakes. It is therefore a collecting field in which knowledge is critical, and there are fewer websites that answer this need. The following, however, should help:

www.speel.demon.co.uk/other/aandc.htm
Arts and Crafts Movement

Overall rating: ★ ★ ★ ★			
Classification:	Arts & Crafts	**Readability:**	★ ★ ★ ★
Updating:	Occasional	**Reliability:**	★ ★ ★ ★
Navigation:	★ ★ ★ ★	**Speed:**	★ ★ ★ ★

UK

Bob Speel, who is clearly very interested in Pre-Raphaelite and Victorian art in general, has this section of his website dedicated to the Arts and Crafts Movement of the 1880s and 1890s.

SPECIAL FEATURES

From this page, there are links to features on all the best known names of the period, such as **William Morris**, **William de Morgan**, **Walter Crane** and so on. There is also information about the Century Guild, the Art Workers' Guild, and the Guild and School of Handicraft founded by **C.R. Ashbee**. The approach is to give information rather than pictorial illustrations, but the material is well written and reliable.

Visiting **Home** within this website, or the **Background Information** link, will take you into much more general explorations of nineteenth century art.

The somewhat solemn approach does not detract from the usefulness of the information here.

www.nga.gov/feature/nouveau/nouveau.htm
National Gallery of Art

Overall rating: ★ ★ ★ ★			
Classification:	Art Nouveau	Readability:	★ ★ ★ ★
Updating:	n/a	Reliability:	★ ★ ★ ★
Navigation:	★ ★ ★ ★ ★	Speed:	★ ★ ★ ★

US

The National Gallery in question here is the one in Washington DC, and this website offers a serious introduction to the subject. It explores an exhibition organised at the Gallery in conjunction with the Victoria & Albert Museum in London.

SPECIAL FEATURES

For once, the layout of the site is logical and progressive. If you start by exploring **Concept** on the homepage, you are transported to two interviews, one with Paul Greenhalgh of the V & A, and the other with D. Dodge Thompson, chief of exhibitions at the National Gallery. The **Introduction** link goes to a fairly brief basic article, while **Timeline of the Art Nouveau Period** is a useful way of relating developments in Art Nouveau to events in the world at large at that period. It ends abruptly, of course, with the assassination of Archduke Ferdinand in Sarajevo.

Audio Tour of Selected Art Nouveau Objects is worth exploring, even if you don't want to download the RealPlayer software, as the images can be enlarged and some brief information about each item can still be read online. The other two areas of the website, **Design** and **Construction**, relate to the practicalities of mounting the exhibition.

Incidentally, this is presumably the same exhibition as was displayed at the V & A from April to July 2000. Irritatingly, the website for that event, with booking details and information about likely queueing times, was still on the web in March 2001! Surely a national organisation could get round to removing its out-of-date pages.

This is a valuable introduction to the subject, even though detail on individual areas, such as Lalique glass, is limited.

www.innotts.co.uk/~jimbobs/culture/nouveau.htm			
James' Art Nouveau Section			
Overall rating: ★ ★ ★			
Classification:	Art Nouveau	Readability:	★ ★ ★
Updating:	Occasional	Reliability:	★ ★ ★
Navigation:	★ ★ ★ ★	Speed:	★ ★ ★
UK			

Nottinghamshire-based James Hinds describes himself as 'a bit of a culture-vulture' and has assembled here some worthwhile information about Art Nouveau, with a welcome focus on the objects as much as the paintings or poster designs.

SPECIAL FEATURES

Despite numerous mis-spellings, it is clear that James has a real interest in the subject. He starts with a brief overview of the origins of Art Nouveau. Below this, but still on the homepage, are **My Art Nouveau Links**, including one to information about the glass designer Emile Galle, another about Charles Rennie Mackintosh, and a third to an extensive exploration of Art Nouveau glass in general, found within the Glass Encyclopedia (see p.84).

This website is not extensive but is still worth a look, and may in due course expand.

OTHER SITES OF INTEREST

arts & crafts movement

Arts and Crafts Society
http://arts-crafts.com
This is the website of The Arts & Crafts Society (in the USA), which subtitles itself 'An online community dedicated to the philosophy and spirit of the Arts &Crafts Movement.' **Archives** is the link for those who want to know more about what the Arts & Crafts movement was.

Antiques World (see p.13) has a good feature on Arts and Crafts Movement Furniture by John Andrews. The route is via **www.antiquesworld.co.uk/Editorial/artscrafts_furn.html**

The Arts and Crafts Movement
www2.uwindsor.ca/~carlone/anc.html
Chris Carlone has a personal website here with a little additional information about Morris, Voysey and Mackmurdo.

art nouveau

Yahoo
http://uk.dir.yahoo.com/arts/art_history/periods_and_movements/art_nouveau/

Here, the search engine **Yahoo** has a special feature devoted to four of the great artists who illustrate the Europe-wide spread of the Art Nouveau style, Aubrey Beardsley, Antonio Gaudi, Gustav Klimt and Alphonse Mucha.

Butterfields
www.butterfields.com/areas/areasleft2.html
This site offers a more informative, though still brief article about Alphonse Mucha.

Dave's Art Nouveau Page
http://members.aol.com/fiawol/nouveau

Dave's Art Nouveau page offers art that is indeed 'nouveau' – in other words, contemporary artists working in the Art Nouveau style, some well, some less well. If you like the style, it might be worth a look, on the chance of picking up a modern treasure. Within the website is a link to the so-called **Mucha Museum**, which turns out to be at Gallery Jizaido in Japan, run by Kyoko Mori. Many examples of Mucha posters can be viewed online, either as part of the museum collection or for sale. In the case of the latter, of course, prices are quoted in yen.

Note: Two other useful sources of information are the Porcelain and Ceramics section of this Guide, starting on p.104, where the entry for Tile Collector (see p.105) is especially relevant; and the Posters section, starting on p.110.

art deco

Global Art Deco Directory
www.lattimore.co.uk/deco/
The Dealer Directory is extensive and is presented alphabetically by name of Shop/Dealer. Back issues of the now discontinued ezine are available to read online. The real value here is in the Links to Other Sites – an excellent list.

Art Deco Fairs
www.artdeco-fairs.co.uk
Up-to-date information about these specialist fairs, which are held regularly in Loughborough. It's a cheerfully stylish site and it also has a feature on the period from the 1950s to the 1970s, entitled Retro Dealers.

Deco Dealers
www.decodealers.co.uk
Amusingly introduced by the Crabtree sisters, Frances, Doris and Beatrice, it lists dealers specialising in Art Deco. The **Sales Arcade** link takes you to where you might be able to make an online purchase.

autographs and letters – antique

Collecting antique or historic autographs or letters (as opposed to contemporary) is certainly a valid and interesting field but not one that is as yet very easy to pursue over the internet. As good a general entry point as any is probably via the famous genealogy gateway site, **Cyndi's List** (**www.cyndislist.com**), where there is a section devoted to autographs. Whereas the most desirable autographs in the past might have been those of members of the Royal Family, politicians, writers, inventors or scientists, today the emphasis has changed completely. Now, almost the only autographs collected in large numbers are those of sports stars or film stars. In this connection, it will be worth looking also at the section on Sporting Memorabilia, starting on page 124. It has proved difficult to find websites that offer good advice or information for collectors, as opposed to websites simply offering to deal, with the exception of the sites that follow:

www.roydavids.com			
Roy Davids Ltd			
Overall rating: ★ ★ ★ ★ ★			
Classification: Dealing		**Readability:**	★ ★ ★ ★ ★
Updating: Regular		**Reliability:**	★ ★ ★ ★ ★
Navigation: ★ ★ ★ ★ ★		**Speed:**	★ ★ ★ ★
UK			

Roy Davids, former head of manuscripts at Sotheby's, has run his own business since 1994. His website tops our list because, as well as the items he is selling, he provides good information about the whole field of autograph collecting.

SPECIAL FEATURES

The link titled **Articles** is particularly well worth exploring. One of these, **The Sacred Duty to Get it Right**, is a profile of Roy Davids himself, while most of the other articles are by him, being either contributions to journals, the text of talks or, in several instances towards the end of the list, poems. Anyone new to the autograph collecting world should certainly start here.

For purchase of manuscript items, this is certainly a most interesting source, though be warned that many of the documents for sale are in the three and four-figure category. Indeed, at the time of writing, a letter with the massively bold signature of Queen Elizabeth I was for sale at a cost of £22,000 + VAT. The quality of the collection is impressive. The left-hand column index divides it under categories such as **Art, Literature, Music** and **Science**, which makes searching very easy.

On its more-or-less-vellum background, this is an elegant, tidy website by a true expert, someone you feel it would be interesting to meet.

www.dmoz.org/Recreation/Collecting/Autographs			
DMOZ Open Directory Project: Autographs			
Overall rating: ★ ★ ★ ★			
Classification: Information		**Readability:**	★ ★ ★
Updating: Periodic		**Reliability:**	★ ★ ★ ★
Navigation: ★ ★ ★ ★		**Speed:**	★ ★ ★
US			

The Open Directory Project relies on a 'vast army of volunteer editors to create the largest human-edited directory of the web.' Visiting this particular page, you are offered a list of some two dozen links, all relevant to Autograph Collecting.

SPECIAL FEATURES

Here it is simply a matter of picking out what looks like a possibly interesting link and trying it. The list includes, for example, the **In-Person Autograph Guide**. This claims to be the 'best and largest guide to authentic examples of autographs that exists.' A subscription (currently $24.95) gives you online access to the Guide for a year. It is very evident from the list as a whole that the emphasis in the USA, at least, is on collecting the autographs of sports stars, film stars and other celebrities rather than, say, writers, scientists or politicians. Be warned that some sites have a tendency to hijack you with advertisements.

This is probably of limited value to the UK-based collector, though some of the success (and failure) stories told by autograph hunters may prove instructive.

OTHER SITES OF INTEREST

Paper Antiques

www.paperantiques.co.uk

Paper Antiques is a general gateway to the whole field of collecting paper memorabilia.

Julian Browning Autographs

www.autographs.demon.co.uk/index.html

This is the website of Julian Browning, a dealer in antique and historical letters and other documents. Typically there will be upwards of 1,000 items for sale at any one time and, although movement around the site can be a bit slow, descriptions are very thorough and detailed. The quality of the collection is excellent.

John Wilson (Autographs) Ltd

http://manuscripts.co.uk

John Wilson, formerly manager of the manuscript department at Maggs Brothers in London, now runs his own business from Painswick in Gloucestershire and this website. Again, collectors will find here large numbers of high quality, historic autograph letters. The system here is that he gives brief index entries in the first instance, with a click on an individual name being the link to more extensive details.

Antique Paper and Ephemera X-change

www.apex-ephemera.com

This is the Antique Paper and Ephemera X-change, an American website which, as well as dealing in paper antiques, offers you a subscription to **Paper Collectors' Marketplace**, a monthly magazine. It is delivered as hard copy, not online, so UK subscribers would have to take postage costs into account.

Note: See also the entry for Roger Gross in the Music section on page 101; and the Leisure Galleries entry in the Transport section on page 136.

autographs and letters – contemporary

An alternative pursuit is, of course, the popular 'sport' of collecting the autographs of the currently or recently famous. This is widely supported on the internet, and **Ebay** (see p.38) in particular seems to sell large numbers of autographs. Websites worth exploring in this connection include the following:

Dave's UK Autograph Website

www.users.globalnet.co.uk/~davhop/default.htm

Dave Hopkins is a Cornwall-based enthusiast who has posted his own site here, concentrating on collecting the autographs of stars of stage and screen. The links from the homepage to **About Me** and **News + Stories** give a good picture of the world of the dedicated autograph collector. He recommends another website, called **Andrew's Autograph Heaven**, and there is a link to this from Dave's homepage.

Autograph Addicts

www.autographaddicts.co.uk

This is a selling forum, listing the autographs in a menu under headings such as UK Actors A-L, US Actresses M-Z and so on. Smaller categories include Glamour, Miscellaneous and Sport.

Autograph Gallery

www.autograph-gallery.co.uk

The clapperboard introduction makes it clear that the emphasis here is definitely on the world of entertainment, though **History** and **Sport** do make small appearances.

Autographs Ink

www.autographs-ink.com/default.html

Here is a UK-based dealer, with a well organised website that also lists forthcoming specialist fairs and auctions.

Autograph Club of Great Britain

www.acogb.com

This is the website of the Autograph Club of Great Britain.

Autograph Collector

www.autographcollector.com

Autograph Collector is an American magazine which can be 'sampled' online.

Cannylink Internet Guide

www.cannylink.com/antiqueautographs.htm

This is another American website with a list of nearly 40 links of interest to autograph hunters.

Memorabilia UK

www.memorabilia-uk.co.uk

Here is a somewhat flashy British website dealing in autographs under the headings **Music, Actors, Politics & Business** and **Sport**.

Autographica

www.autographica.co.uk

This is the website of Autographica, The World's Largest Autograph Show, being held in 2001 in Northampton, England. Apart from information about the Show itself, Lotsa-Links is probably the most useful part of the site for further exploration.

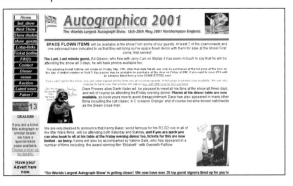

books

Collecting Antiquarian Books is a field in which the internet really comes into its own. For many collectors, using the internet is simply an extension of collecting by mail, which has long been an accepted method anyway. Previously, they received posted catalogues; now they can search infinitely more sources online. One reason why this works is that an antiquarian book either is, or is not, what it claims to be, in the sense that the defining characteristics of a first or early edition are hard to fake. The condition of books being sold remains an issue, as always, but accurate descriptions of the condition of old books have a terminology all their own, and collectors have long accepted the assurances of reputable book dealers and ordered or not, accordingly.

The following three websites all enable you to search for antiquarian books online:

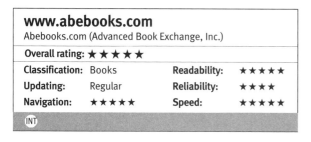

www.abebooks.com

Abebooks.com (Advanced Book Exchange, Inc.)

Overall rating: ★ ★ ★ ★

Classification:	Books	Readability:	★ ★ ★ ★ ★
Updating:	Regular	Reliability:	★ ★ ★
Navigation:	★ ★ ★ ★ ★	Speed:	★ ★ ★ ★ ★

(INT)

Despite its now international scope, this is still a heavily UK-used and -influenced website, as well as an outstandingly good source for any serious book collector.

SPECIAL FEATURES

The **Quick Search** facility is the largest feature on the homepage, and it can be used immediately, with no need to log in first. The search allows you to specify Title, Author, Keyword or Publisher, and results are quickly delivered in a very reader-friendly form. In a test case, the same search that produced six titles when put to Biblion conjured up over thirty hits in Abebooks. Some of these were American, admittedly, and one was in Tokyo, but most were still to be found in the UK. The ordering system, once you have found a book you want, is clear and straightforward.

Other features available from the homepage will normally include a profile of one particular bookseller, as well as some recent book news or feature articles. Pursuing these may well lead to very useful additional information. For instance, the **Maps and Prints** link, if followed through, produces a very good article on this specialist collecting field by Joel Kovarsky, as well as a dedicated search facility.

The **Let Us Search For You** link does require membership, which is free. **Our Features Page** will lead you not only to the article of the moment, as is indicated on the homepage,

but also to several others, on topics such as sci-fi or romantic fiction.

Collector's Corner, right at the bottom of the homepage, has a slightly quirky feature that you may find useful. Below whatever is the feature article of the moment is a photograph of a single bookshelf loaded with apparently well-used, mostly Victorian books. You can either browse these 'blind', so to speak, clicking on one that takes your fancy (the spines are mostly unreadable), or you can use the helpful link below and see them all individually. They all prove to be books about book collecting, a clever enticement!

Learn More About Book Collecting! looks like another promising link but the seminars to which it refers are all, for the time being at least, held in the USA.

Definitely a winner when it comes to searching for rare, out of print or simply interesting books.

www.addall.com			
AddALL			
Overall rating: ★ ★ ★ ★			
Classification: Books		**Readability:**	★ ★ ★ ★ ★
Updating: Regular		**Reliability:**	★ ★ ★ ★
Navigation: ★ ★ ★ ★		**Speed:**	★ ★ ★ ★
(INT)			

This is another major bookselling forum, this time claiming to search the others: Abebooks, Alibris, Antiqbook, Bibliofind, Biblion, Biblioroom, Half.com, Just Books and Powell's Books. As they say, 'Why waste your time going from site to site? You can search all of them with just one click.'

The claims mentioned above are true, it seems, and the search facility works well. It is important to note that the search facility offered on the homepage is for books currently in print, not antiquarian books. This is something that might be very useful if you are seeking to compare prices, especially as the results may include special trade editions. Results are listed in order, cheapest first.

SPECIAL FEATURES

To search for antiquarian or second-hand books you need to click opposite the question **Searching for Used Books?** This takes you to another page, where a new search facility is offered. If you are simply using the facility to compare prices, perhaps to identify the value of a book you already own, then you only need to change the entry in the currency box to UK£, the last option in the drop-down list.

This earns a very slightly lower rating than Abebooks, because there are no features or articles about book collecting as a pursuit, but it is still a most valuable resource.

www.biblion.co.uk			
Biblion			
Overall rating: ★ ★ ★ ★			
Classification: Books		**Readability:**	★ ★ ★ ★
Updating: Regular		**Reliability:**	★ ★ ★ ★ ★
Navigation: ★ ★ ★ ★		**Speed:**	★ ★ ★ ★
(UK)			

'The home of British antiquarian and remarkable books', Biblion is a main source for antiquarian book collectors (and sellers) on the internet.

SPECIAL FEATURES

Before making use of all areas of this website you will need to log in, an easy procedure initiated near the top of the right-hand margin. Only those fields with a star beside them have to be filled in. Log-in is instant.

There are numerous links on the homepage (which, even if you enter 'co.uk' in the URL, will still come up as '.com', incidentally), among them a useful one to **ABm's Auctions/Fairs Calendar**, in other words Antiquarian Book Monthly's forthcoming events.

Other links include a feature article entitled **The Essentials of Book Collecting**, a detailed explanation of how to approach antiquarian book collecting by the American book dealer and author, Robert F. Lucas. This is an excellent introduction to the topic. Meanwhile the index on the blue panel to the right of the homepage lists various specialist collecting interests, such as **Signed Limited First Editions**, **Leather Bindings**, **Cricket Books** and so on.

Other links will be available from the homepage, including whatever are the specially featured books on the date you visit. If you want to search for a book, however, you should use the search box in the page-header. As the system here is relatively simple, you need to give as much information as you can. For example, putting in 'The Waves' produced all titles in which the word 'waves' appeared; putting in 'Virginia Woolf' produced 232 titles, including not only all books available by her but also all those about her; so putting in all four words, 'Virginia Woolf The Waves' was the route to reducing the list to just five. These complications would be avoided by using the **Advanced Search** link, in the bar below the header, instead.

Certainly a prime site for anyone interested in antiquarian book collecting.

boxes

Whether the collecting of boxes really deserves a section all to itself is debatable. On the other hand, box collecting is very popular, ranging from the tiniest of pill-boxes to quite large boxes, such as unfolding writing desks. It is not a difficult interest to pursue on the internet, if you are looking to buy, as most boxes are relatively easy to pack and post safely. Checking condition and quality may be a problem and here you are, as with most 'distance' purchases, in the hands of the seller. The only significantly useful website in terms of offering information, as opposed to items merely for sale, appears to be Antique Boxes, reviewed overleaf.

www.users.globalnet.co.uk/~boxes/boxweb/index.html			
Antique Boxes			
Overall rating: ★ ★ ★ ★ ★			
Classification:	Boxes	**Readability:**	★ ★ ★ ★ ★
Updating:	Regular	**Reliability:**	★ ★ ★ ★ ★
Navigation:	★ ★ ★ ★	**Speed:**	★ ★ ★ ★ ★
UK			

Sewing boxes are particularly featured here, though tea caddies, jewellery boxes, glove boxes, writing boxes and snuffboxes are all detailed as well. As the illustrations show, many of these have great charm and are highly collectable, though these days usually expensive.

SPECIAL FEATURES

The website owner, Antigone Clarke, has written a good page entitled Antique Boxes in English Society, accessed from the link in yellow on the homepage as **The Online Antique Box Book**. It is best to start by reading her **Introduction** before selecting the particular type of box that interests you. There is a very interesting article on the topic of faked tea caddies near the top of the index, and another on the connections between tea and the opium trade.

At the time of writing the promised page on **Conservation/Restoration/Care** was not yet available but, given the level of expertise displayed throughout the website already, it should prove very valuable.

A beautiful, elegant website, presented by a true expert.

carpets and rugs

Carpets and Rugs can be objects of great beauty and value but few purchasers are sufficiently knowledgeable to identify the different types of rug correctly, let alone know whether what they are being offered are genuinely good examples. Once again, knowledge is a paramount necessity if you propose to collect or deal in rugs. It is so easy to be misled as to the age or the value of a carpet or rug, so it is important to buy from respected sources and, before you buy, to inform yourself as thoroughly as possible. The following websites would not claim to offer anything like a comprehensive tutorial in this fascinating collecting field, but they will get you started.

http://home.earthlink.net/~gordsa		
RugLore		

Overall rating: ★ ★ ★ ★ ★			
Classification: Carpets/rugs		**Readability:**	★ ★ ★ ★
Updating: Occasional		**Reliability:**	★ ★ ★ ★ ★
Navigation: ★ ★ ★ ★ ★		**Speed:**	★ ★ ★ ★ ★

US

www.turkotek.com		
Turkotek		

Overall rating: ★ ★ ★ ★ ★			
Classification: Carpets/rugs		**Readability:**	★ ★ ★ ★ ★
Updating: Regular		**Reliability:**	★ ★ ★ ★
Navigation: ★ ★ ★ ★ ★		**Speed:**	★ ★ ★ ★ ★

UK

88-year-old Sam, the owner of RugLore, calls this 'an information resource for all with a love for rugs.' It is effectively a non-commercial, online magazine, with masses of writing and no illustrations. Don't let that put you off.

SPECIAL FEATURES

The homepage is divided into two headings; Current Articles and Past Articles. There is a lot of reading here, if you have the patience, but there is no question that Sam knows his stuff and loves his rugs.

Under Current Articles you will find **Introduction to Buying and Selling**. The terrors of trying to buy at auction, described under Buying, might be enough to deter you from even attempting to engage in this sport. Prices quoted are, of course, in dollars. **Selling** is equally full of dire warnings but contains many good tips too.

The Lure of the Antique gives Sam the opportunity to sound off about what he calls 'antiques mania', while **Dyes** is a very informative explanation of how dyes are produced and how the development of synthetic dyes affected the carpet trade.

If you need more information about rug collecting, buying and selling than you find here, then good, old-fashioned books are your only resort.

Turkotek describes itself as 'a non-commercial site devoted to collectible weavings, where rug enthusiasts can connect.'

SPECIAL FEATURES

The first area to explore is Archive, where articles include **Why are Birds Depicted Like that on Rugs?** and **The Oriental Rug as a Work of Art**. Further down the list is **The Language of Carpets**, **Dating Tribal Rugs** and **How is a Repaired Rug Valued?**

Attribution Guides are divided into four types, namely Chodor, Salor, Tekke and Yomut. Clicking on **Articles** produces nearly twenty features, including one by Steven Price entitled **Are Oriental Rugs Good Investments?**

From **Links** you obtain another good and extensive list, well worth exploring. There are also numerous opportunities for sharing information about rugs and weavings, including **Discussion Boards** and **Virtual Show and Tell,** where enthusiasts can post pictures of their treasures and share information.

This is a most attractive website, dedicated to informing rather than selling.

OTHER SITES OF INTEREST

Cloudband
www.cloudband.com

Arcade is the selling arm of Cloudband, while **Gallery** introduces current exhibitions. **Magazine** leads to the company's own publication, describing itself as 'the definitive online magazine for carpets, textiles, the arts of Asia and tribal art.' **Discussion** is a question and answer forum, while **Listings** is a calendar of events. **Links** offers a good list, organised into categories that are shown on the right of the screen. Most of those listed under **Resources** connect to websites of general Asian art interest, rather than to sites dedicated to carpets and rugs, however.

Samarkand Galleries
www.samarkand.co.uk

Brian MacDonald collects and sells especially the tribal rugs of the Near East and Central Asia. His website allows you to view many beautiful rugs, to find out about his book and lectures, and to explore some interesting links.

Oxford Decorative Arts
www.eurorugs.co.uk

Among the more interesting of the dealers with an online presence is Oxford Decorative Arts, who specialise in twentieth century European rugs, many by named designers. The shop is actually in London. A thumbnail catalogue of rugs currently in stock can be viewed online and clicking on any image brings up a larger picture and a brief description. Prices are not given but an online enquiry form is provided.

cartoons

The collecting of cartoons falls into two basic categories. You can either seek to collect the original work of the cartoon artist, which might be something as simple as a pencil drawing scribbled on the back of an envelope, or you can collect cartoon art as originally published. Both these kinds of collecting overlap, inevitably, with other areas covered within this Guide. The original artwork by a cartoonist may well be found in the same sort of area as autographs and paper ephemera, while published cartoons are certainly closely related to the world of collecting comics, or periodicals such as 'Punch.' Meanwhile Debbie Weiss's website, detailed below, specialises in animation art, a slightly different cartoon-collecting field again.

www.animationartcollecting.com
Animation Art Collecting

Overall rating: ★ ★ ★ ★ ★			
Classification:	Animated art	**Readability:**	★ ★ ★ ★ ★
Updating:	Regular	**Reliability:**	★ ★ ★ ★ ★
Navigation:	★ ★ ★ ★ ★	**Speed:**	★ ★ ★ ★ ★

UK US

Debbie Weiss writes regularly about animation art for the UK magazine 'Collectables' as well as for the American journal 'Animated Life'. Allowing for a two-month delay, articles from those two magazines are then republished on her website in full.

SPECIAL FEATURES

Articles include **Different Types of Animation Collections**, **Ten reasons why NOT to buy Animation Art** and so on. The writing is peppy and accessible, and the illustrations within the articles or in Debbie's Online Gallery, **Wonderful World of Animation**, are good. There are plenty of opportunities for using the site interactively, emailing Debbie with suggestions for future articles, for instance, or telling her about your own collection.

Enjoyable, larky and yet seriously informative too, this can't be bettered when it comes to animated art.

OTHER SITES OF INTEREST

Cartoon World
http://work.winbiz.co.uk/iwm14/customhtml2/
Cartoon World may be worth some exploration. Certainly it has details of cartoon events and exhibitions, and the fact that all this is presented spaciously, on a white background, is a relief. The ordering of the information isn't as clear.

Mark J Cohen – Original Cartoon Art
www.markomics.com
The website of Mark J. Cohen, American enthusiast and collector, contains quite a bit of helpful information about collecting cartoons under FAQs, linked from the question mark logo at the bottom of the page.

The Telegraph
www.telegraph.co.uk/00/3/1/ixgall.html
This is a feature that appeared in the Daily Telegraph, on Wednesday 1 March 2000, about the British Cartoon Centre's exhibition 'The 100 Cartoonists of the Century.' Below the introductory paragraph (and a savage Mrs Thatcher cartoon) are links that allow you to **View the Cartoons** or find out **About the Cartoonists**. Unfortunately the details given about the cartoonists are minimal in the extreme but better than nothing.

The Cartoon Art Trust
www.atreides.demon.co.uk/docs/natmus.html
The Cartoon Art Trust has its website here, with three links available from the homepage: **Training Courses**, **The Gallery** and **Joining the Trust**. The Trust's objective is to collect and conserve cartoon art, eventually establishing a National Museum of Cartoon Art, but no information about this aim, nor about the great artists of the past such as Hoffnung, Thelwell or Calman (all mentioned on the homepage) is available here. In fact very little information is available online but at least contact details are given.

cinema memorabilia

Collecting Cinema Memorabilia embraces more than just collecting photographs and autographs of the stars. For those, in any case, you will do better to consult the Autographs and Letters section of this Guide from p.57. Similarly, although the websites below certainly cover cinema advertising and posters, you may also like to look at the Posters section on p.110. If, on the other hand, you want to broaden the range of your cinema collecting interests, try the following for ideas and further information:

www.ex.ac.uk/bill.douglas/menu.html			
The Bill Douglas Centre for the History of Cinema and Popular Culture			
Overall rating: ★ ★ ★ ★			
Classification:	Cinema	Readability:	★ ★ ★ ★
Updating:	Regular	Reliability:	★ ★ ★ ★
Navigation:	★ ★ ★ ★	Speed:	★ ★ ★ ★
UK			

Some areas of this website, such as **Tour of the Collection**, are being redesigned but it is still an impressive resource.

SPECIAL FEATURES

Virtual Exhibitions includes features on Hitchcock, D.W. Griffith, Houdini and Charlie Chaplin, as well as material about the precursors of cinema, such as magic lantern shows and other optical entertainments. Clicking on any of these leads to a further set of links that expand on the topic in question. The information is verbal rather than pictorial.

Teaching & Learning introduces the courses available at Exeter University, where the Centre is located. The best explanation of the Bill Douglas Centre's function is found here under **Online Articles and Web Pages by Staff and Students**, where Duncan Petrie's report for the magazine 'Screen' is published in full.

Finally, **Related Websites**, linked from the bottom of the film-reel index on the homepage, offers an excellent list that will generally reward exploration. It includes lists of **Film Museums and Collections**, among them a link to the National Museum at Bradford.

For background information about the history of cinema, this is excellent, though it is not specifically a guide to memorabilia for collectors.

MEM Music & Cinema Memorabilia
www.memcollect.co.uk

The proposal here is to make this the premier site in the UK for cinema memorabilia. The collection, of over 60,000 items, is currently being catalogued in two sections: **Music/Vinyl Catalogue** and **Cinema/Poster Catalogue**. Much work is needed, so it is impossible to assess the quality of this website yet.

Dublin's Cinemania
www.clubi.ie/cinemania

Dublin's Cinemania is a real-world store dealing mainly in current or recent films, but there are fine collections of posters and magazines (most illustrated here online) dating back to the early days of cinema, and this makes a good, informative resource for the collector.

Netribution
www.netribution.co.uk

Go to **Links** and then **Film Related Products** and finally **Posters** or **Memorabilia** for massive lists of (mainly dealer, mainly US) websites.

clocks and watches

This is another big collecting field, ranging from the most imposing grandfather clock to the smallest of jewelled watches. It is also one that takes the collector far back in history, because it has always been of such importance for people to be able to know the time, and the clocks they made to tell them were therefore objects of value, much treasured. How shocked some of the early makers, who created timepieces of such precision and beauty, would be at the idea of mass-manufactured disposable watches of the sort quite common today.

http://duke.usask.ca/~lowey/watches/index.html		
As Time Goes By		
Overall rating: ★ ★ ★ ★ ★		
Classification: Watches	**Readability:**	★ ★ ★ ★ ★
Updating: Regular	**Reliability:**	★ ★ ★ ★
Navigation: ★ ★ ★ ★ ★	**Speed:**	★ ★ ★ ★ ★
US		

www.bhi.co.uk/index.html		
The British Horological Institute		
Overall rating: ★ ★ ★ ★ ★		
Classification: Clocks	**Readability:**	★ ★ ★ ★ ★
Updating: Regular	**Reliability:**	★ ★ ★ ★ ★
Navigation: ★ ★ ★ ★ ★	**Speed:**	★ ★ ★ ★ ★
UK		

Kevin Lowey is watch-obsessed, but despite his regular reminders that he is an amateur, not an expert, he certainly knows his stuff.

SPECIAL FEATURES

The links from the homepage include **Watch Collecting**, **What's Your Watch Worth?**, **Watch Identification**, **How Watches Work** and **Watch History**. All of these lead to very informative articles by Kevin, along with onward links to other websites that expand on the topic in question. The unfamiliar term at the bottom of the homepage index, **Remove Menus**, links to a list of websites Kevin has consulted for his own information.

More information about Kevin Lowey is available from a mass of links under his name in the index. These include **Full Frontal Nerdity**, from which you may indeed feel he cheerfully suffers, given how much stuff he has put on his website!

Watch collecting, even with the somewhat American slant to be expected from a US collector, is explored here in rewarding detail.

The British Horological Institute's homepage offers **Site Index** as one of its many starting points. If you click here and scroll right to the bottom of the resulting page, you will immediately get an idea of the almost daunting amount of information here.

SPECIAL FEATURES

This is an amazingly detailed and valuable website, as you will discover as soon as you start exploring. The **General** link in the left margin introduces you to some of the functions of the Institute, with **About the BHI** (founded in 1858) as a good starting point. Now, returning to the homepage, try **Technical** for some thoroughly practical information about clocks and clock care. In this area, **Hints & Tips** is apparently the link most visited.

Other Sites takes you to a list you could spend days exploring! It includes links to the **BWCCA** (British Watch and Clock Collectors Association), a list of well over forty non-commercial links, and somewhere in the region of a hundred commercial ones. It ends with **Mailing Lists & Discussion Groups**.

This website demonstrates how extraordinarily rich the internet can be as a source of information – but don't let's forget that any website of this sort only exists because some intelligent person has spent a great deal of time assembling and marshalling that information.

www.clockswatches.com
Historical Clock and Watch Research

Overall rating: ★ ★ ★ ★			
Classification:	Timekeeping	**Readability:**	★ ★ ★ ★
Updating:	Regular	**Reliability:**	★ ★ ★ ★
Navigation:	★ ★	**Speed:**	★ ★ ★ ★

UK R £

This may well be, as they declare, 'The Best Research Site for Clocks and Watches!' The need to subscribe to view the whole site (see below) is what reduces the star-rating above.

SPECIAL FEATURES

Access to the illustrations of clocks (which are provided by individual collectors) in **Photograph Gallery** is only available on a subscription basis, currently £3.00 for 24 hours' viewing. The same applies to **What's New** and **Archive Library** at the top of the homepage. All subscriptions go into enhancing this non-profit website. If, however, you are prepared to write a page about a particular clock maker, you will be 'paid' with a day's free access. Meanwhile, the two **Bulletin Boards**, one dedicated to **Research** and the other to **Repairs**, are open to all and the questions, answers and follow-ups are very informative.

A prime site but one where you would do well to have the list of research topics you are exploring well worked out before subscribing.

OTHER SITES OF INTEREST

MEM D Phillips Company
www.pond.com/~pdp/
Paul D Phillips is a knowledgeable dealer in Philadelphia, USA. His website gains its place here mainly because of a good introductory article, 'Some Thoughts on Collection Clocks', which would be a good starting point for any collector. The term 'flee (sic) markets' presents a whole new concept to the imagination!

The Horological Foundation
www.antique-horology.org
The Horological Foundation maintains this 'meeting and trading plaza' online and it deserves some exploration. **Articles** is as yet thin in material, with only two items so far available, one of which compares the work of Thomas Tompion and Joseph Knibb. **Collections** links to a list of countries, with Great Britain being a further link, and thence to a good list of clock collections in museums around the country.

Collecting Clocks
http://web.ukonline.co.uk/collecting-clocks
Collecting Clocks heads a simple homepage with a few links highlighted in blue, most leading to Barrie's Virtual Museum of Clocks (also available from **www.clock-museum.co.uk**). This is a good website for viewing examples of different types of clock, though the range shown in each category tends to be limited.

It's About Time
www.clocking-in.demon.co.uk
This is the website of the cleverly named It's About Time, an established Antique Clock dealer based in Essex, with good pictures of clocks, and a little additional information.

coins

Coin collecting, as opposed to 'numismatics' which also includes medals, is another very popular collecting field. Rather like stamp collecting, it has particular appeal for young collectors, who can start small in terms of both scope of collection and value of individual items. Oddly, though, it is an area where information online is distinctly thin on the ground. You can access dealers and 'swappers' certainly, but access to practical information is more difficult. There are other areas of this Guide in which you should look, however. One is under Militaria, beginning on p.95, because some medal collecting websites also have links to information about coins. Another is under Silver, on p.119.

www.tclayton.demon.co.uk
Tony Clayton's Home Page

Overall rating: ★ ★ ★ ★			
Classification:	Coins	Readability:	★ ★ ★ ★ ★
Updating:	Regular	Reliability:	★ ★ ★ ★
Navigation:	★ ★ ★ ★ ★	Speed:	★ ★ ★ ★ ★

UK

Retired physics teacher, Tony Clayton, has his own friendly website here, with good information for any UK-based numismatist.

SPECIAL FEATURES

Metals used in Coins and Medals is a fascinating article for those who wish to know more about the elements and alloys from which coins are made. The other links from the homepage are **Coins of the UK,** which starts as far back as the Norman Conquest, **Decimal Coins of the UK,** and **Values of UK Coins** (extremely useful). Any of these lead to very well indexed further pages. Tony does, incidentally, have an interest in **Machin Stamps of the UK and Italy** as well.

Links at the bottom of the homepage leads to a list of only a dozen or so, some of which are Tony Clayton's own articles already linked above, but they are still worth exploring. They include **Guernsey Coins** and **Irish Coins.** The link to **Paul Lewis's page on UK Coins** takes you to an article entitled 'What's a Guinea?', very helpful for anyone who is not clear about how pre-decimal coinage in Britain worked.

Much the best introduction to the subject for anyone collecting British coins. Only Tony's own disclaimers prevent the reliability rating being five-star as well.

OTHER SITES OF INTEREST

The British Numismatic Society
www.fitzmuseum.cam.ac.uk/coins/britnumsoc/index.html
The British Numismatic Society has what is, for the time being, a very basic website giving details of what the Society does and nothing else. At least it tells you where to contact them, though they are not available by email.

The British Coin Collector
www.britishcoincollector.co.uk
The British Coin Collectors' Site is mainly aimed at people who want to sell and/or swap coins, and practical information about coin collecting as a pursuit is not great, but there is a useful link to **Auctions**.

Marron Coins & Sheffield Coin Auctions
www.marroncoins.co.uk
Marron Coins & Sheffield Coin Auctions have a website that gives little peripheral information but is useful if you wish to find out about forthcoming auctions.

Coin News
www.coin-news.com
Coin News is Britain's principal coin magazine. You can't read it online but you can take out a subscription, having viewed a list of topics in whatever is the current issue of the moment.

Coin Today
www.cointoday.com
Coin Today is the American equivalent of Coin News, with the difference that it can be read online. The articles under **World Coins** may be especially well worth exploring.

costume

In the early stages of compiling this Guide, Costume didn't have a section to itself but was included along with Textiles and Soft Furnishings. It soon became plain that it deserved its own area, but if you are interested in costume you should still look at that section too (see p.130). Costume is an extremely fascinating field for the collector, and one in which there are still some relatively disregarded items that could still be assembled into interesting collections for relatively little cost. The example given in the website below is a good one.

http://members.aol.com/nebula5/costume.html			
The Costume Page			
Overall rating: ★ ★ ★ ★			
Classification: Costume		**Readability:**	★ ★ ★ ★ ★
Updating: Ceased		**Reliability:**	★ ★ ★ ★
Navigation: ★ ★ ★ ★ ★		**Speed:**	★ ★ ★ ★ ★

US

Although mainly aimed at those who want to re-create authentic historic costumes, there are good links here. The approach is highly informative but largely non-pictorial.

SPECIAL FEATURES

Julie Zetterberg Sardo in Seattle is the owner of this website. The first five sections on her homepage, with titles all beginning **The Study of Costume**, are likely to be of most interest to collectors. To take just one example, under **The Study of Costume – Historical Topics** is a section headed **Male Attire**. This leads to a list of a dozen further links, one of which is **Turn-of-the-Century Hard Collars and Cuffs**, a neat, explanatory article by Tara Maginnis who collects such collars and is able to keep her entire collection in a biscuit tin. Even then, by the way, you haven't exhausted the possibilities this website has to offer, as there are still a couple of further highly relevant links to tell you more about collars. So one way or another this is a very dense source of information, intelligently ordered.

It is true that there tends to be a North American bias to the websites selected, as the main message of the website as a whole is addressed to US-based enthusiasts wishing to study and re-create costumes of the past. But this is by no means exclusively the case, as will be seen if you explore the links thoroughly.

The Study of Costume – Costume History is centred on Western/European dress and starts from Ancient Clothing, including good material on Roman dress, before moving through Medieval and Renaissance periods. There is particular strength in the 19th Century Regency and Victorian Era. There is also a large section on **The Study of Costume – Ethnic & Folk Costume**.

This is a wonderfully rich website. The tragedy is that in February 2001 it carried an announcement in red to the effect that, due to time restrictions, it was no longer going to be updated. Let's hope either someone else adopts it or time is found!

OTHER SITES OF INTEREST

Living History
www.livinghistory.co.uk
Living History is a portal to a number of websites dealing in historic costume, more aimed at those involved in historical re-enactment than at collectors.

A Century in Shoes
www.centuryinshoes.com
You can still view this website, A Century in Shoes, without the Flash technology plug-ins by clicking on **No Flash Entry**. There is a preliminary page of historical information available from the **Before This Century** link at the bottom of the page. Having looked at that, you can now explore the shoes of the twentieth century decade by decade, using the 'time-clock' at the top right-hand corner of each page.

ephemera and packaging

Defining ephemera on its own is not perhaps as straightforward as it might seem, especially today when throw-away items are more plentiful than ever. The most elegant definition is the one given by The Ephemera Society (see p.76) but even that leaves something of an open question, because where do 'documents' begin and end? What today we call a flyer or a leaflet, and in the past was perhaps a broadsheet, intended to be disposable, is certainly a document. So, one supposes, is a bus ticket. But what about the paper or thin card used to wrap a packet of tea? Is that a document?

In the end, the easiest solution seemed to be to put the two together (which stretched the definition even further because that meant including tins too) and hope that no purists would be too offended. Enthusiasts will want to look at the information to be had from the Postcards and Posters sections (see pp.108-111), and possibly in the Magazines and Periodicals section too (see p.90).

www.paperantiques.co.uk
Paper Antiques

Overall rating: ★ ★ ★ ★			
Classification:	Ephemera	**Readability:**	★ ★ ★ ★
Updating:	Regular	**Reliability:**	★ ★ ★ ★
Navigation:	★ ★ ★ ★	**Speed:**	★ ★ ★ ★

UK

This website correctly describes itself as 'the best resource for collectors and dealers of paper antiques, ephemera and memorabilia.' It is consequently worrying to see that the homepage has a red notice across the bottom saying that the website is for sale.

SPECIAL FEATURES

The trading side of the website is indexed to the left of the page, the information side mainly to the right. **Links** leads to a good list of other websites of relevance to paper antiques collectors. From **Site Archive** you will find some special features that have appeared at earlier dates on this website, and related books. The **Library Archives** listed at the foot of the right index, on the other hand, are those of other organisations.

Also in the left index are lists of **Collectors**, **Dealers** and **Auctions**, all well organised. Meanwhile, much time can be very pleasantly spent trawling around the **For Sale** area of the website, needless to say!

Though principally a commercial website, the visible involvement of the various dealers and collectors, and such things as the question and answer area, make it informative too.

Wicked Lady

www.wickedlady.com

Go to Wicked Lady and click on **Tins**. This takes you to The Tin Pages, with links to **Collectors** and **Dealers**, but also to **Biscuit Manufacturers, Tin Box Manufacturers, Printing Processes** and plenty of illustrations.

The Museum of Advertising and Packaging

www.themuseum.co.uk

Robert Opie (whose parents were Iona and Peter, famous collectors of nursery rhymes) himself collected packaging tins and boxes, and advertisements. His collection is now The Museum of Advertising and Packaging in Gloucester, the only one of its kind in the world. His website is as yet fairly primitive, but anyone really interested in the history of packaging needs to know of the Museum's existence. At the bottom of the homepage there is a link to his other website, **Nostalgic Images**, where you can order reproductions.

Ephemera & Paper Collectibles

www.hobby-collectibles.co.uk

Ephemera & Paper Collectibles is a good place to look for such things as **Playing Cards, Cigar Box Labels, Luggage Labels** and **Cigarette Packets**. There are also sections on **Black Americana** and **Magic**. The information lies as much in the illustrations as in any text.

The Ephemera Society

www.ephemera-society.org.uk

The Ephemera Society preserves and studies 'the minor transient documents of everyday life', an elegant way of saying 'things that most of us throw away.' Apart from the homepage details of the Society itself, the only link here is to **Ephemera Fairs**. You can also fill in an online form to apply for membership, which brings access to lists of members and their interests, and the quarterly journal, The Ephemerist.

ethnic art

The definition of Ethnic Art has been used here in rather general terms, firstly to cover any non-Western art, and secondly to cover objects as well as fine art. One result is that this section therefore also includes oriental art. Putting the words 'oriental antiques' or 'orientalia' into any good search engine will of course instantly, with no problem at all, produce a range of alluring websites, filled with entrancing pictures. It is much more difficult to find practical advice for would-be collectors. On the other hand, the illustrations in these websites are often so good as to form a valuable resource in themselves.

In general, this is an area of the internet very much dominated by American, and some Japanese, websites, with the emphasis consequently tending to be on the arts of the Americas or Asia. From the Folkart.com website described on p.77, however, you will find some links to most areas of ethnic and folk art worldwide, including Europe and Australasia.

http://asianart.com
asianart.com

Overall rating: ★ ★ ★ ★ ★			
Classification:	Ethnic Art	Readability:	★ ★ ★ ★ ★
Updating:	Regular	Reliability:	★ ★ ★ ★ ★
Navigation:	★ ★ ★ ★ ★	Speed:	★ ★ ★ ★

US NEP

Pictorially exquisite, this truly is an online gallery of Asian art.

SPECIAL FEATURES

The four main links from the homepage are to **Associations**, such as the Kathmandu Valley Preservation Trust and the Tibet Heritage Fund; **Exhibitions**; **Articles**, including features on everything from Chinese snuff bottles and Wangden meditation weavings in Tibet to the Bangladeshi arts of the ricksha (sic); and **Galleries**, which lists dealers worldwide and is almost undoubtedly the best list you will find anywhere.

The real value of this website lies in its wealth of information, the object being to enhance the study of Asian art in all its forms. **Exhibitions** is a link to a calendar of online exhibitions, which one could happily spend hours 'visiting.' A different list of actual, real-world events is found under the **Departments** link, and then **Calendar of Events**. In this same section you will find both **Letters** and **Forum**, where articles by visitors to the website are posted, some pretty arcane, many very interesting. Finally, look at **Asianart.comBookstore** and Links, which are divided by country.

Unquestionably the first port of call for anyone interested in Asian Art.

www.folkart.com
Folk Art & Craft Exchange

Overall rating: ★ ★ ★ ★			
Classification:	Ethnic Art	Readability:	★ ★ ★ ★ ★
Updating:	Regular	Reliability:	★ ★ ★ ★
Navigation:	★ ★ ★ ★ ★	Speed:	★ ★ ★ ★

US

Latitude International, a Californian company, is in the business of promoting the appreciation of folk art and craft throughout the Americas. It's a commercial operation, certainly, and UK-based collectors would find purchasing from the USA and importing items expensive, but the website is so thorough and informative that it earns its place here regardless.

SPECIAL FEATURES

The homepage menu is lengthy, with first a list of forty countries all over the world to choose from, and then a list nearly twice as long of categories, including **Baskets**, **Quilts** and **Furniture** among many others. It is basically a showcase for the dealers concerned, but simply by viewing the artefacts one can learn a lot and many links contain information as well as pictures.

Especially informative is the online **Art & Culture Newsletter**, available from a link at the top right of the homepage. Meanwhile at the bottom of the homepage, just above disturbing pictures of youngsters posted by the National Center for Missing and Exploited Children, are links to **Private Art Collections**, **Links to Museums** and **Folktales**.

A fascinating website with extraordinary breadth.

www.crowcollection.com
The Trammell & Margaret Crow Collection of Asian Art

Overall rating: ★ ★ ★ ★ ★			
Classification:	Ethnic Art	**Readability:**	★ ★ ★ ★
Updating:	Regular	**Reliability:**	★ ★ ★ ★ ★
Navigation:	★ ★ ★ ★ ★	**Speed:**	★ ★ ★ ★

(US)

This whole website is an exercise in perfectionism. The Museum itself is, perhaps rather unexpectedly, in 'the Arts District of downtown Dallas'. Its collections are exquisite.

SPECIAL FEATURES

Visitor Information tells frustratingly little and might justly be described as 'inscrutable'. The Collection leads to three symbols, against the links **Type, Period** and **Culture**. These refer to ways in which the collections can be 'visited.' Type, for example, offers such choices as **Hanging Scrolls**, **Screens & Panels** and **Personal Use & Adornment**, while Culture and Period are both arranged by country. If Period is the sifting mechanism of choice, then a second set of options will appear, referring to whatever are the relevant periods within the country selected. Eventually, each choice will lead to a list of actual objects, from which you select some to view. Many are offered with 3D rotational viewing, if you have the appropriate plug-in. They are also all displayed with good explanatory comments.

Galleries produces a computer-generated interior view of each gallery, which enlarges when you click. By now you will have a list of the regions covered in that gallery, and a further click brings up lists of objects. It is all very intriguing, though perhaps not the quickest method of finding your way around, but if you are still determined to explore the mysteries of website wizardry you can now try the **Virtual Tour**.

Asian Cultures is divided into **Region**, which brings up a map of Asia where you can select by clicking on the relevant country and read an essay, while **Religion** produces the same map and a helpful key to identify which religions predominate where, again with essays. All this is presented with extreme elegance and sophistication, but such exquisite refinement means either that you need a lot of time or a very powerful computer.

Calendar of Events refers to the Museum's own events, while under **Education** you will find **Links to Other Sites**, where once again you start by selecting a country. The ensuing lists are excellent and range worldwide.

You could spend almost as long touring the Crow Collection online as you might spend on a real-life visit, so beguiling is this luscious website.

www-sul.stanford.edu/depts/ssrg/africa/art.html			
Africa south of the Sahara			
Overall rating: ★ ★ ★ ★			
Classification:	Ethnic Art	Readability:	★ ★ ★ ★ ★
Updating:	Regularly	Reliability:	★ ★ ★ ★
Navigation:	★ ★ ★ ★	Speed:	★ ★ ★ ★
US			

This is an intelligent assembly of links to relevant websites, listed on a single page and with good descriptions of what will be found in each.

SPECIAL FEATURES

It would be impossible to list here all the topics this website covers, but it begins with **African Textiles** and ends with **Zimbabwe Stone Sculpture**. The **Search** facility, top-left of the page below the header, enables you to interrogate the list in different ways, by country or by topic. **South African Art** is a second feature, to which there is also a link.

It would be hard to better this website for the access it offers to information about African Art. It is only because it is limited in scope to this one function that it earns such a modest overall star-rating.

OTHER SITES OF INTEREST

Art Information on the Web
www.library.csustan.edu/lboyer/art/art.htm
Art Information on the Web: Selected Sources. This gateway has good links to a number of art resources, including features on North American Art and, under the link **Web Museum: Famous Paintings Exhibition**, good material about Japanese artists.

Chinese Art
www.chinese-art.com
This portal website gathers and sorts information about Chinese art, both traditional and contemporary.

Engelen.com
www.engelen.com/links/ethnicart.html
Belgian artist, Leon Engelen, is chiefly online here to attract buyers for his oil paintings, but has assembled an excellent list of links to other art websites, including this short list of ethnic art resources.

A Piece of Africa
www.a-piece-of-africa.com
The information here via **History of African Art** is especially well worth exploring. The company, A Piece of Africa, operates from both England and South Africa.

Native American ArtPages
www.kstrom.net/isk/art/art.html
This is a prime site for the exploration of Native American Indian Art. Its use is straightforward and the articles it contains are exceptionally interesting.

Aboriginal Art
www.aboriginalart.com.au
This is a good site for viewing examples of Aboriginal art, along with good background information available from the **Culture** link at the bottom of the page.

Aboriginal Fine Arts Gallery

www.ozemail.com.au/~hallpa/indexb.html

This is another prime site for viewing Aboriginal art, being the internet's largest online gallery of such work. There are also links to **Artists' Profiles** and **Aboriginal Culture**.

Folk Archive

www.folkarchive.co.uk

Folk Archive is an ongoing project to collect and display folk art from all over Britain. There is an online opportunity here for you to notify the Archive of examples of contemporary artists working in the true folk art tradition.

fans

This collecting interest is, admittedly, a fairly confined one, although the range of fans that can be collected is perhaps wider than many people would assume. It is a field where repair, conservation and display are all absolutely critical, and the main website detailed here is a good source of information on such matters.

www.hand-fan.org
International Fan Collector's Guild

Overall rating: ★ ★ ★ ★			
Classification:	Fans	Readability:	★ ★ ★
Updating:	Ceased	Reliability:	★ ★ ★ ★
Navigation:	★ ★ ★ ★	Speed:	★ ★ ★ ★

US

Cheryl Melnick, who says she spent ten months creating this website for the FANA (the Fan Association of North America) only to have her efforts turned down, is annoyed! Fortunately for fan enthusiasts, she decided to post it on the web anyway.

SPECIAL FEATURES

From the homepage you need to click on **Site Map** to explore this website in full. Even though **Resources** is probably the area that is going to be of most interest, there are links available from the main list that are worth exploring too, such as **Fan Tours** and **History of Fans**.

Under **Resources** you will find **Language of the Fan**, **Styles of Fan** and **Preservation** among others. **Media** is also well worth consulting.

Unfortunately this website is for sale and is no longer being updated, so the most recently added material, which you will find below Cheryl's tirade on the homepage, dates from March 2000.

Despite some difficulty in reading the yellow print against a black background, this website is well worth your time – even allowing for the fact that it is no longer being updated.

OTHER SITES OF INTEREST

Antique Fans
www.antiquefans.freeserve.co.uk
Carol Desler, who can be contacted by email, is a collector and dealer in London. If you wish to view some antique fans in close-up detail, often with good written descriptions too, her website will really delight you. **Spanish Fans** and **Chinese Fans** have sections to themselves, but Fan-related Items is as yet very limited.

fireplaces

Numerous websites with ingenious names such as Old Flames and Grate Expectations are to be found by putting the words 'antique fireplaces' or 'period fireplaces' into a good search engine, but the results invariably turn out to be the websites of dealers. All too often, in fact, the fireplaces in question are only reproductions of antique or period designs anyway. Unfortunately, very little appears to be available in terms of information about either the history of fireplaces, or their most famous manufacturers and designs. Below is the only website that seems to be of any help, not one that really merits a major entry. If anyone out there knows of something better, please let the Good Web Guide know!

British Fire Service

www.fire.org.uk

At the website of the British Fire Service there is a look at the historical development of fire safety regulations. Be warned, though, that it contains numerous mis-spellings such as 'medievil, slowley, disasterous' and so on. You will find the link under 'Fire Safety & Fire Engineering', entitled **History of Fire Safety Legislation in the UK**. Meanwhile, under 'Miscellaneous', in a blue bar well down the homepage is a link to **Memorabilia Collectors Page**. It is not very informative but it does give a list of enthusiasts with very brief details of what they collect or sell, and email contact addresses.

furniture

This one was a surprise. You might expect that there would be countless resources on the internet giving information about furniture, in terms of the evolution of designs, the great furniture-makers and so on. In fact, there is an almost complete blank. Perhaps the problem is that the internet is better suited to dealing in the small items marketplace. It may indeed be true that very few serious collectors are going to buy items as major as pieces of furniture over the internet, though that doesn't deter the furniture dealers from advertising, as you will see if you search simply for 'antique furniture' websites. So why is there so little material available to help the collector looking for instruction?

The only really useful website appears to be the one detailed. Otherwise, you can only search the general-purpose websites listed at the beginning of this guide, or visit The British Association of Furniture Restorers' website (see p.49).

www.iserv.net/~plucas/

FM4

Overall rating: ★ ★ ★			
Classification: Furniture		Readability:	★ ★ ★ ★ ★
Updating: Regular		Reliability:	★ ★ ★ ★
Navigation: ★ ★ ★ ★		Speed:	★ ★ ★ ★

US

Pamela Lucas, frustrated that there was no website that gathered together furniture resources on the internet, decided to create one herself. As Pamela is Michigan-based, it is no surprise that the majority of furniture and decorative arts dealers mentioned in her website are American.

SPECIAL FEATURES

Click on **Styles and Periods** under Furniture History and you will move to a list of informative websites, ranging from **Furniture Design** to a virtual tour of **The Mackintosh House**. There's also a **Glossary of Modern Terms**, starting with **Art Deco**, **Bakelite** and **Bauhaus**, and ending with two modern American designers, **Edward Wormley** and **Russel Wright**.

Museums & Exhibits and **Regional Furniture Styles** are other areas of the website worth exploring, though the emphasis here is heavily on American collections. Under Furniture Design, the first link is to contemporary American designers but **The Eminent Designers** ranges worldwide. You need to understand French to read the **Articles About Furniture**, as they are all taken from issues of the French magazine, Art & Décoration.

As indicated above, this appears to be the best furniture-dedicated website currently available. Its predominant focus on American furniture certainly should not deter any furniture enthusiast from exploring it.

glass

Glass collecting is a field in which novice or inexperienced collectors often feel somewhat at sea, whether collecting the humblest of glass bottles or the finest examples of the glass-maker's art. The marks that identify glass as being from a particular country or period are much more elusive than those on porcelain, for example. One approach, and one that can of course be applied in all collecting fields, is simply to collect what appeals to you for its beauty and not worry about its provenance. On the other hand, many collectors feel a natural wish to learn more about their treasures and, of course, the very difficulty of correct identification means that great finds can still be made if you know what to look for. Accordingly, it may be very important, and beneficial, to consult those websites that help with the identification process.

www.glass.co.nz
Glass Museum On Line

Overall rating: ★ ★ ★ ★ ★			
Classification:	Glass	Readability:	★ ★ ★ ★ ★
Updating:	Regular	Reliability:	★ ★ ★ ★ ★
Navigation:	★ ★ ★ ★ ★	Speed:	★ ★ ★ ★ ★

NZ

This is a beautiful website, clear, informative and well organised. Its New Zealand origin does not stand in the way of its usefulness to UK-based collectors.

SPECIAL FEATURES

There are so many links available here that there is no possibility of doing this website justice in a few words. Try **Glass Encyclopedia** as your first area of exploration. Then move well down the homepage, below the book recommendations and the link to **The Paperweight Connection**, until you reach the wonderful list of articles available for reading online. These include features on **Art Deco French Glass**, **British Glass after the War**, **English Carnival Glass**, **Opalescent Glass**, **Crackle Glass** and many more.

Even then, you have by no means exhausted the possibilities. Near the bottom of the homepage is an invitation to explore the **Links Page**. Inevitably there is something of a New Zealand emphasis here, but it is still worth having a look.

Five-star in every respect.

www.great-glass.co.uk
Great Glass

Overall rating: ★ ★ ★ ★ ★			
Classification:	Glass	Readability:	★ ★ ★ ★ ★
Updating:	Regular	Reliability:	★ ★ ★ ★ ★
Navigation:	★ ★ ★ ★ ★	Speed:	★ ★ ★ ★

UK

Philip and Ann Petrides are glass dealers, displaying their wares either online or at various fairs around the country. They have put together a highly informative website.

SPECIAL FEATURES

Their own stock is displayed first, under **Shop Windows**, divided into four periods, **Before 1900, pre-War, post-War** and **Pressed Glass**. Below this is **Glass Notes**, where you will find a **History of Glass** (fairly condensed), details of **Manufacturers' Labels & Marks, Cleaning & Restoring Glass** and other topics. **Decanters & Drinking Glasses** is a handy short-cut method of identifying types, very clearly illustrated with outline drawings. Loading of the pages is a little slow in this area.

Almost the most useful part of the whole site is found in the **Links**, a remarkably practical list. It includes a route to **The Glass Encyclopedia**, a New Zealand website that features an extraordinary range of different types of glass (see previous entry), and at the bottom of the page also lists **Antiques & Collectors Fairs** at which the Petrides themselves exhibit.

Start here for anything to do with glass, certainly. The information is clear and reliable without being patronising.

www.antiquebottles-glassworks.co.uk
Glassworks of Gloucester

Overall rating: ★ ★ ★			
Classification:	Bottles	**Readability:**	★ ★ ★
Updating:	Regular	**Reliability:**	★ ★ ★ ★
Navigation:	★ ★ ★ ★	**Speed:**	★ ★ ★

UK

Given its location, in the restored Gloucester Docks, it is not surprising that this website looks particularly at the bottle-types and bottle-makers of that area, but there is good general information here too.

SPECIAL FEATURES

The homepage has a short introduction to the Glassworks company, below the picture, and then two areas of blue boxes. In the first block the boxes all transfer you to examples of the bottle-types in question, listing items currently for sale and illustrating many examples. The photographs are excellent but do cause each page to load quite slowly. Don't miss the **Links** box, though, because the ensuing list is one of the best you will find. Other features available from the bottom row of boxes include **Show Diary** and **About Us**, the story of how the website owner, Paul Best, became obsessed by bottle-collecting.

The second block of boxes is smaller, with some links to histories of local bottle companies, two glossaries to **Codd** and **Ginger Beer** bottles, and a very helpful **UK Bottle Terminology** link. It is a pity that these, in smallish coloured print on a brown background, are not easier to read.

A well-conceived website for anyone interested in old bottles, with good onward links to other helpful sources.

OTHER SITES OF INTEREST

Just Glass
www.justglass.org.uk
Colin Smith, of The Glassblowing Workshop, is a glass blower and repairer working at St Andrew's University, and a member of the British Society of Scientific Glassblowers (link available from his homepage). His own website, still being developed, is strictly practical, explaining much about the techniques of glassblowing. Visit his links page, **Other Glassblowers**, especially those to **East Carolina University**, for glassblowing tips, and the **Corning Museum of Glass**, in New York State, USA.

International Paperweight Society
http://selman.com/ips.html
The International Paperweight Society has a smart website here, though the **Featured Artists** are all contemporary, not makers from the past. **Trivia** is an amusing link, reminding us that France, asked to display French craftsmanship at the Great Exhibition of 1851, chose paperweights. Learn About Paperweights is only a partial link; actually to 'learn more' you need to sign up for free information. Below the form, you will find that you can even send a free **Paperweight Greeting Card**, accompanied by music ranging from John Dowland's Pavane to Great Balls of Fire!

Christine Bridge Antiques
www.antiqueglass.co.uk
This is the website of Christine Bridge Antiques, so well illustrated that it deserves mention, even though it is a purely commercial forum. Georgian, Edwardian and other types of glass are all generously covered.

James Hetley & Co
www.hetleys.co.uk
James Hetley & Co sells stained glass supplies, but here you will also find a good list of websites from which to pursue an interest in stained glass. Click on **Contact** and then **Links**.

Finesse Fine Art

www.fine-art.demon.co.uk/Lalique/lalart.htm

Although Tony Wraight's main interest is specifically the glass car mascots of René Lalique, he has a very good article here about Lalique in general, as well as about the 29 mascot designs. There is also a link to the dealing arm of the operation, selling mascots as well as other motoring accessories.

Historic Glasshouse

www.antiquebottles-glass.com

Historic Glasshouse is a good, quick American website with lots of information and various links, though the emphasis is, obviously, directed at US-based bottle-hunters.

Note: Some of the websites included in the Porcelain and Ceramics section of this Guide, starting on page 104, also feature glass. Finally, on page 144 there is a link within the Wine section to the Antique Wine Bottle and Black Glass Collectors' Club.

jewellery

The search for independent websites about jewellery collecting, as opposed to dealers simply selling, was disappointing. Plenty of books on the topic are recommended but there is relatively little that can be read about the subject online. Probably the best general information about jewellery is to be found from within the pages of Ebay (see p.38), where there is an article about the History of Jewellery by Arthur Guy Kaplan and good links to topics such as Factors that Influence Value, Displaying or Storing Jewellery and Caring for your Jewellery. Others among the gateway websites, like the BBC Online – Antiques (see p.15) may be of help too.

www.alvr.com
A La Vieille Russie

Overall rating: ★ ★ ★			
Classification:	Jewellery	**Readability:**	★ ★ ★
Updating:	Regular	**Reliability:**	★ ★ ★ ★
Navigation:	★ ★ ★ ★	**Speed:**	★ ★ ★

US

This prime, Fifth Avenue dealer has a very attractive website, with so many examples of Russian jewelry (American spelling, note) illustrated that it is informative in that way alone.

SPECIAL FEATURES

Russian jewellery is of exquisite design, if sometimes excessively ornamental for the restrained British taste. Putting up with the small print, do explore here the **News, Articles & Publications** area of the homepage index, and enjoy in particular the features on Imperial eggs.

If Russian jewellery is your favourite, gorge the senses here.

OTHER SITES OF INTEREST

About Antiques: UK
http://uk.antiques.about.com/aboutuk/ukantiques/cs/jewellery
Within the pages of About.com is this page, with a handful of jewellery links, mostly to commercial websites. The **Caveat Emptor – Buyer Beware** link is certainly worth a quick read.

lighting and lamps

While there may not be many people who are in the business of assembling lamp collections as such, the right choice of lamp can be critical in terms of creating an atmosphere in a room. Many frustrating hours must have been spent by lovers of the period look, searching for the lamps that will enhance rather than destroy the effect. Information about what lamps belong to what periods, how particular lighting effects were achieved, and how lamps were used in the past will always help in that quest.

www.antiquelamps.net
Antiquelamps.net

Overall rating: ★ ★ ★ ★			
Classification:	Lighting/Lamps	**Readability:**	★ ★ ★ ★ ★
Updating:	Regular	**Reliability:**	★ ★ ★ ★ ★
Navigation:	★ ★ ★ ★ ★	**Speed:**	★ ★ ★ ★

(US)

David O Benson has put together just about the only really good website on lamps and lighting, in terms of information, that was found.

SPECIAL FEATURES

The focus here is on early, pre-electric lighting, including special features on **Banquet Lamps, Table Lamps, Glass Lamps** and others. **History of Lighting** is a short but articulate essay, and **Resources** leads to a selection of books on the subject. There is also an introductory link to **Light International**, a new magazine actually published in the UK.

Don't fail to explore also the **Antique Lighting Webring**, available from a link at the bottom of the homepage. **List Sites** is the quickest way into this directory.

For the antique or period lighting enthusiast, this would seem to be the best available.

OTHER SITES OF INTEREST

The Hutchinson Family Encyclopedia
http://ebooks.whsmithonline.co.uk/
Enter the world lamp in the first search box and there is an article here on very early lamps, starting with prehistoric stone lamps. It only comes as up-to-date as the post-Roman period, but it is well written and interesting.

Peter Noonan, Purveyor of Oil Lamps
www.oil-lamps.co.uk
Peter Noonan both restores and sells old lamps. His website has some good illustrations and, at the foot of the homepage, an article on **Care and Safe Operation of Oil Lamps**. He also sells spare parts.

Mike's Electric Stuff
www.electricstuff.co.uk
An 'anorak' site, but if you want to know about things like **Mercury Arc Rectifiers and Geissler Tubes**, Mike's Electric Stuff will tell you.

Pairs Antiques
www.pairsantiques.co.uk/items/lighting/lighting.htm
Specialist dealer, Pairs Antiques, will normally have some attractive lighting items for sale, Even though information is limited, it is still somewhat frustrating that the descriptive information about illustrated items is withdrawn once they are sold, even though their pictures remain online.

The Historical Lighting Society of Canada
www.historical-lighting.on.ca
The Historical Lighting Society of Canada may be worth exploring, more for its onward links than for the site itself.

luggage

It is only in fairly recent years that old trunks and leather suitcases, as well as smaller bags, have started appearing as important features in antiques dealers' displays and auction-house showrooms. Today, even a somewhat battered leather suitcase, defaced by the remnants of the stick-on labels that used to indicate where its owner had travelled and monogrammed with that owner's initials, can fetch a large sum of money. Sometimes, such items sell to those wishing to complete the country-house picture artificially being created of a long-used tack or boot-room. But there are collectors who love leather goods simply for their intrinsic, sturdy beauty. These websites may be of use to them.

www.casehistory.co.uk
Case History

Overall rating: ★ ★ ★			
Classification:	Luggage	**Readability:**	★ ★ ★ ★
Updating:	Regular	**Reliability:**	★ ★ ★
Navigation:	★ ★ ★	**Speed:**	★ ★ ★

UK R

This ingeniously named website was still in development at the time of writing, though what was already online looked promising.

SPECIAL FEATURES

The link entitled **History** for the moment only takes you to a short quiz in which you can test your knowledge. **Exclusive** involves filling in an email address to obtain further information and is therefore effectively a restricted area of the website that cannot be properly reviewed here. The **Links** are as yet rather too general to be of specific interest to luggage collectors.

This website needs to keep growing, hence the as-yet modest star-rating.

magazines & periodicals

Listed here are websites of interest to those collecting magazines, periodicals and comics from the past. This is a major collecting field, especially given the vastly increased value of 'complete runs' as opposed to sets from which a few issues are missing. If all you need is a back issue of a recently published or current magazine, you will do better looking in the Journals section of this Guide.

www.bl.uk/collections/newspaper/collect.htm			
Collections : The British Library Newspaper Library			
Overall rating: ★ ★ ★ ★			
Classification: Periodicals		**Readability:**	★ ★ ★ ★
Updating: Regular		**Reliability:**	★ ★ ★ ★ ★
Navigation: ★ ★ ★ ★		**Speed:**	★ ★ ★ ★
UK			

The prime source in the UK for finding information about periodicals and comics.

SPECIAL FEATURES

Select the **Periodicals and Comics** link and then, **British Comics Collection**. This will lead to five further links, of which the **History of the Collection**, **Scope and Highlights of the Collection** and the **Select List of British Comics** will probably prove the most rewarding.

Another valuable area of the periodicals collection is **Victorian Illustrated Newspapers and Journals**. This, however, is a guide to what the collection contains rather than any detailed information being made available online. New areas being covered by the periodicals collection and now also featured online include **Pop and Jazz Music, Cinema and Film** and **Football**. Again, these are lists of holdings rather than extensive online information.

This is unquestionably the right place to do research, if you can get to the Library in person. The need to do so, rather than the possibility of gaining the information online, is what governs the star-score above, not any question about the Library's credentials.

http://comicbookannuals.tripod.com

J.R. Chapman Comic Book Annuals

Overall rating: ★ ★ ★			
Classification:	Magazines/Periodicals	Readability:	★ ★ ★ ★
Updating:	Regular	Reliability:	★ ★ ★ ★
Navigation:	★ ★ ★	Speed:	★ ★ ★ ★

UK

This is a top website for the study of British comics or annuals.

SPECIAL FEATURES

J.R. Chapman's website – no doubt sensibly – conceals his full name or whereabouts, as his **Private Collection**, detailed in full here, must obviously be valuable. Certainly, he's a British collector ('.co.uk') and his website is excellent. The list under **Annuals** in the left-hand menu is very comprehensive, though each link only takes you to copies of issues for sale. Meanwhile, just above it, the **Links** in particular (which also give details of forthcoming events) and the **Articles** are worth a visit. The last of the Articles, **Collecting Comics**, is by J.R. himself.

Thanks mainly to the links, which are extensive, this is a good starting point for anyone collecting comics or annuals.

OTHER SITES OF INTEREST

Wellesley Index to Victorian Periodicals
www.routledge.com/electronic/wellesley/contents.html
Any serious researcher will sooner or later want to consult the Wellesley Index to Victorian Periodicals. It is not available for consultation online but it can be bought as a CD-rom (for significant money) or consulted in libraries. A useful part of the website is found from the bottom of the homepage, where there are two most useful links: The first is to **Victoria**, the Victoria Research Web based in Indiana. The second is to **SHARP**, the Society for the History of Authorship, Reading and Publishing – also American but with lots of non-American links to such useful resources as the **Internet Library of Early Journals**.

Uni-net Leisure and Hobbies – Comic Collecting
www.uni-net.co.uk/leisurehobbies/collecting/comics.html
There are half a dozen links here, including one to **Astérix & Tintin** and another to **Peanuts** (via the Comics.com link), with a little additional information, such as a profile of Charles Schulz.

Collecting Comics
www.collectingcomics.com
This website – which clearly should be of relevance for collectors – has been notified and is in the process of being developed, though at the time of writing there is nothing available.

maps & prints

One of the oldest-established collecting fields, this is also one where fakes are common, especially with all the techniques available today for reproducing the authentic look. Genuine old maps, along with such items as early globes, are scarce and have great value. Disreputable dealers have not been slow to see the opportunities and, unfortunately, many beautifully produced books have been taken apart or had their illustrations stolen, for subsequent sale as if they were individual prints. The temptations to perform this sort of desecration are great when a single leaf from an illuminated manuscript can command a four-figure sum. The collector should therefore do everything possible to ensure the authenticity of what he or she is buying.

Other areas of this Guide that may contain websites of use to the print collector are Ephemera, starting on p.75, and Posters on p.110.

www.rare-maps.com
Art Source International

Overall rating: ★ ★ ★ ★			
Classification:	Maps/Prints	**Readability:**	★ ★ ★ ★ ★
Updating:	Regular	**Reliability:**	★ ★ ★ ★
Navigation:	★ ★ ★ ★ ★	**Speed:**	★ ★ ★ ★ ★

US

This American website will be of value to any serious collector of maps, simply for the breadth of information it contains.

SPECIAL FEATURES

The index in the left-hand margin helpfully appears on every page. The place to mine for real nuggets of information about how to acquire or care for maps is **Collectors Guide**, found under **Site Tools**. Here, an introductory article fills the centre of the page, with a whole host of sub-links on the right. These include **What is Meant by the Term 'Antique Map'**, **Factors Affecting Value** and **How to Detect Reproductions.** Two other sections on this page explore the **History of Print Making** and offer **Time Charts of Historical Cartography**.

Other features in the main index include **Antique Prints** and **Vintage Posters** (these turn out to be reproduction vintage posters). Scanning the images will reveal that the majority of topographical prints are American, but the site as a whole is well organised and easily used. **Medieval Manuscripts** is another main-index feature and here genuine leaves from illuminated psalters and the like are offered for sale, at significant prices.

This website has plenty to recommend it from the information point of view, even if it is of less interest to UK-based collectors who wish to purchase.

<table>
<tr><td colspan="2">http://ihr.sas.ac.uk/maps
Map History/History of Cartography</td></tr>
</table>

Overall rating: ★ ★ ★ ★ ★			
Classification:	Maps	**Readability:**	★ ★ ★ ★ ★
Updating:	Regular	**Reliability:**	★ ★ ★ ★
Navigation:	★ ★ ★ ★	**Speed:**	★ ★ ★ ★ ★

UK

Tony Campbell of the British Library maintains here what he claims, rightly, is 'THE Gateway to the subject.'

SPECIAL FEATURES

The only problem here is the densely small print on the homepage. Try not to be put off, because using any of the links in the index immediately moves you to much more easily read pages. **Map Collecting** might be the best place to start, where you are immediately offered a whole host of onward links, including one to an article by Joel Kovarsky, hosted by AbeBooks and entitled 'The Allure of Old Maps' and another by Dee Longenbaugh, 'Primer for the Beginning Collector of Maps.' A third link goes to the website of Dutch specialist, Paulus Swaen, with a good article entitled 'Tips for Prospective Map Collectors'.

Another feature linked from the homepage studies **Globes – History,** and there is also much information about the commercial side of map collecting, from fairs and exhibitions to lists of map dealers worldwide.

Certainly a prime source for map collectors, with plenty of information and well organised links.

<table>
<tr><td colspan="2">www.postaprint.co.uk
Postaprint</td></tr>
</table>

Overall rating: ★ ★ ★ ★ ★			
Classification:	Maps/Prints	**Readability:**	★ ★ ★ ★
Updating:	Regular	**Reliability:**	★ ★ ★ ★
Navigation:	★ ★ ★ ★ ★	**Speed:**	★ ★ ★ ★ ★

UK

This is a prime source for the collector of maps and prints in the UK.

SPECIAL FEATURES

This long-established and respected dealer has a tidy website, which includes various helpful features. Practical aspects such as ordering apart, the best of these will be found under **Resources Pages** in the homepage index. Both **The Image Library** and **Site Index,** within this area, is available to any visitor to the website, no registration needed. Images are grouped under subject headings, which are unfortunately explained in very small print. They are only a small, representative selection of the whole collection. Also under Resources is the **On-line Bookshop,** which is merely a link to the online presence of bookseller Barnes & Noble.

Meanwhile, **External Links,** still under **Resources,** is an exceptionally useful part of the website, definitely one of the aspects that earn it a five-star rating. Here you will find links to articles of interest to the collector, as well as a huge list of other websites worldwide, such as Auction Houses, Libraries and Societies. Early in the first list is a useful explanation of the various printing techniques, 'UK: How Antique Maps and Prints Were Printed.'

Search is the other most valuable area of the website, containing a database of over quarter of a million prints and other items for sale, though not all by any means are illustrated. There are also large sections devoted to illustrations that appeared in the magazines Illustrated London News, the link being titled **ILN Database**, and **Vanity Fair**. A clever idea is the **Dated Gifts** Search, where you can search for a print to match the date of an anniversary.

It is also worth exploring the **New Offers** area of the website, since this contains maps and prints not yet entered in the main database. Prices in all areas of the website appear in dollars unless you use the Select Currency button. Ordering involves ticking the order box and then clicking on Add to Shopping Cart at the bottom of the page.

A first stop for the map and print collector.

www.antiqueprints.com

Steve Bartrick Antique Prints & Maps

Overall rating: ★ ★ ★ ★

Classification:	Maps/Prints	Readability:	★ ★ ★ ★ ★
Updating:	Regular	Reliability:	★ ★ ★ ★
Navigation:	★ ★ ★ ★ ★	Speed:	★ ★ ★ ★ ★

UK

Steve Bartrick has been a dealer since 1984 and now has two shops, one in Ross-on-Wye and one in Gloucester. His website lists the prints and maps he has for sale, of course, but is also extremely rich in supporting information.

SPECIAL FEATURES

The first of the links on the homepage all relate to the commercial aspects of the website and are very straightforward to use.

Information is where the meat of the site is, in terms of learning more about map and print production. The onward link **How they were made** is especially valuable in this respect. **Links** is mainly devoted to commercial websites, but starts with a short list of general interest sites, including one to the **International Map Collectors Society** and another to **MapHist,** an email discussion forum for those interested in the history of cartography.

This is so evidently the website of a true enthusiast, it is a joy to explore.

OTHER SITES OF INTEREST

Altea Antique Maps
www.antique-maps.co.uk
Altea Antique Maps is one of the principal online dealers, with an elegantly-designed website. Illustrations are good and load quickly. The very large list of maps for sale makes this a good reference source, though there is no additional information about maps as a field for the collector.

Mercator's World
www.mercatormag.com
Mercator's World magazine, a top journal for map collectors, can be explored here. A newsletter is available for reading online but the magazine itself only exists in full in a bookstall form, though it can be ordered online.

Oddens Bookmarks
http://oddens.geog.uu.nl/index.html
Oddens Bookmarks, based at Utrecht University in the Netherlands, contains over 13,000 cartographic links, including excellent details of map fairs worldwide. Don't worry – it's all in English, not Dutch.

MapForum.com
www.mapforum.com
MapForum.com is an online periodical for antique map collectors. Clicking on any given issue produces a menu. The **Letters** link under **Reader Services** is also worth visiting, as the answers to enquiries are very detailed.

Note: When it comes to collecting contemporary (as opposed to antique) prints, the best approach is through a search engine such as Google. 'Contemporary Prints UK' will produce a list of over 35,000 websites in a matter of seconds. One good source of information, as well as purchases, is **www.kamprint.com/collect.htm**, home of the Kamakura Print Collection. Despite the emphasis on Japanese art, the well-written advice holds good for all print-collecting activities.

militaria & weapons

It doesn't take much surfing to discover that militaria, which includes medal collecting, is a hugely popular collecting field, so selecting websites to mention here is difficult. The vast majority of the items advertised for sale over the internet come from the two World Wars, rather than from earlier periods, though some of the websites here will also be of assistance to those with that interest too. There are rules affecting the possession of weapons, of course, and the last four websites listed all address this issue of legality.

www.german-militaria.co.uk			
German Militaria and Collectables			
Overall rating: ★ ★ ★ ★			
Classification:	Militaria	**Readability:**	★ ★ ★ ★
Updating:	Regular	**Reliability:**	★ ★ ★ ★ ★
Navigation:	★ ★ ★ ★ ★	**Speed:**	★ ★ ★ ★ ★
UK			

Fascinating, super-efficient website doing a great deal more than simply dealing. The only problem at times is the dark background to the pages.

SPECIAL FEATURES

Collecting Militaria, in Background Information, was still under construction at the time of writing but there are lots of other things to investigate. Try **What's New, Information on Medals and Awards, German Aircraft of the Second World War, Third Reich Uniforms and Regalia** or any of the items under **Interesting Articles.** Meanwhile, under Links and Information there are other trails to pursue, such as **Maker Marks & Codes** and **Fakes & Reproductions.** And if you are still not satisfied, have a look at the impressive list under **Assorted Links & Web Rings.** In addition you can order relevant books and find out everything you might need to know about **Restoration & Preservation** of your treasures.

Perhaps this website really has had the more than three hundred thousand visitors it claims (and actually probably deserves) in the last year!

www.arbeia.demon.co.uk			
Militaria On the Web			
Overall rating: ★ ★ ★ ★			
Classification:	Militaria/Weapons	**Readability:**	★ ★ ★
Updating:	Regular	**Reliability:**	★ ★ ★ ★
Navigation:	★ ★ ★ ★	**Speed:**	★ ★ ★
UK			

As yet somewhat limited in scope, this is still a worthwhile effort.

SPECIAL FEATURES

Collectors Guides contains a small selection of articles giving fairly brief details of **British Gallantry & Campaign Medals** and two features on **Edged Weapons** (bayonets). **Military Posters** has a fine collection of well-illustrated examples, but be warned that clicking on any image does not enlarge it, it merely takes you to the Barnes & Noble bookstore. There is a good list of **Military Museums** with contact details but no direct online links. A few, however, can be toured via the alternative link, **Military Museum visits.**

The website's owners admit that they are getting many requests for further information, to which they intend to respond. If they do, this will be very good indeed; meanwhile it remains in the 'could do better' category.

OTHER SITES OF INTEREST

Arms and Armour
www.arms-and-armour.co.uk
Vincent Lody, the owner of this website, has actually put together some of the most helpful practical information for the collector of militaria to be found anywhere on the web. Exploration is so simple as to need no explanation here.

The Lanes Armoury
www.armsandarmour.co.uk
Not to be confused with Vincent Lody's website (see above), this is The Lanes Armoury, a dealer based in Brighton. The website earns its place here due to a good range of illustrations.

Treasure Bunker
www.treasurebunker.com
Treasure Bunker is a Glasgow-based dealer now with a very significant online presence. The homepage link to **The Bunker** tells you just a little about the business, but **Catalogue Index** takes you to an amazingly rich selection of items, any of which can be viewed by clicking on the revolving camera icon. Details are minimal but illustrations are very good.

Medals & Medal Collecting
http://members.tripod.co.uk/hinckley1/medals.html
The first link here is to **Medal Collecting – What's It All About?** and subsequent links, which are then more specific, should tell you most of what you need to know about the various British medals. Below this list are half a dozen links to Other Medal Websites, and then more to medal dealers.

Hargreave Mawson
www.hargreave-mawson.demon.co.uk/Links.html
Any medal collector needs to see this, to explore the excellent list of Links on Mike Hargreave Mawson's page.

Militaria
www.militaria.co.uk
This transports you to some notable dealers but is not an especially information-rich source.

The Militaria Collector's Network
www.users.zetnet.co.uk/lwarren/mcn/home.html
The Militaria Collector's Network is a mailing list forum where you can share your interest with other collectors.

Antique Guns
www.antiqueguns.com
Antique Guns is an American website that may prove rewarding, allowing for the fact that there is likely to be a considerable emphasis on Civil War weaponry. It has a heavily interactive bias.

Armourer
www.armourer.co.uk
Armourer is, as it says, the UK's premier militaria magazine, available only on bookstalls but to which you can subscribe here online. The website offers little, though you can consult a list of back issues with details of contents, and there is also a link to **Dates and Venues of UK Arms Fairs**. The link to **Skirmish** is to a journal aimed at those involved in historical re-enactments. The **Links** at the bottom right of the homepage are mainly to commercial websites (in green uppercase letters) but below them (in blue) are some sites of more general, research interest.

Home Office

www.homeoffice.gov.uk/ppd/oppu/histarm.htm
Here you will find guidance to the police from the Home Office about the issuing of firearms certificates, under Firearms (Amendment) Act 1997: Section 7. It is important for the owners of historic firearms to know which categories are exempt.

HMSO

www.parliament.the-stationery-office.co.uk/pa/ cm199697/cmhansrd/vo961119/debtext/61119-17.htm
and
www.parliament.the-stationery-office.co.uk/pa/ cm199900/cmhansrd/vo000420/text/00420wo2.htm
These are two extremely relevant pages from Hansard, the first from a major debate on 16th November 1996, the second recording a written parliamentary answer on 20th April 2000, relating to who may and may not own historic firearms.

Antique Rules

www.gun.demon.co.uk/antiquerules.htm
More manageable perhaps (certainly as a website address!) is this page, which also outlines the legal situation relating to the ownership of antique weapons.

music & musical instruments

Some areas of collecting have been much more intractable, in terms of finding websites to recommend, than others. One of these, unexpectedly, was music. Admittedly it is a big field, covering everything from early instruments to vinyl records and gramophones, and from sheet music and opera posters to autographs of the famous. Nevertheless, it was surprising that it took two solid days of browsing to sift out even the rather thin list of websites included here. Additional suggestions recommended by readers will be welcome.

<table>
<tr><td colspan="4">www.bubl.ac.uk/link/m/musicalinstruments.htm
BUBL Information Service</td></tr>
<tr><td colspan="4">Overall rating: ★ ★ ★ ★ ★</td></tr>
<tr><td>Classification:</td><td>Music</td><td>Readability:</td><td>★ ★ ★ ★ ★</td></tr>
<tr><td>Updating:</td><td>Regular</td><td>Reliability:</td><td>★ ★ ★ ★ ★</td></tr>
<tr><td>Navigation:</td><td>★ ★ ★ ★ ★</td><td>Speed:</td><td>★ ★ ★ ★ ★</td></tr>
<tr><td colspan="4">UK</td></tr>
</table>

This website wasn't easily found, but it was worth it. BUBL is an information service, based at Strathclyde University, aimed at the 'higher education community', though it holds much of interest for the lay person.

This unfussy, non-illustrated approach may not be particularly striking in web design terms but it does have the virtue of being practical.

SPECIAL FEATURES

There are 16 items in the main menu, ranging from a **Guide to Medieval and Renaissance Instruments** to a **Music Glossary** and several specialist collections of musical instruments. From the top header, however, you can select links to each of the separate areas of the orchestra (brass, percussion and so on) and here there are new indexes, with many more articles to read. All in all, it adds up to a rich source, well catalogued and very easily used.

Have a quick look at Subject Menus at the top of the homepage and you will discover that BUBL actually covers a mass of different areas. Why, during the process of researching this book, it never appeared in a search engine result until 'Music' was the topic remains a mystery.

<table>
<tr><td colspan="4">www.pianola.demon.co.uk
The Player Piano Page</td></tr>
<tr><td colspan="4">Overall rating: ★ ★ ★ ★ ★</td></tr>
<tr><td>Classification:</td><td>Music</td><td>Readability:</td><td>★ ★ ★ ★ ★</td></tr>
<tr><td>Updating:</td><td>Regular</td><td>Reliability:</td><td>★ ★ ★ ★ ★</td></tr>
<tr><td>Navigation:</td><td>★ ★ ★ ★ ★</td><td>Speed:</td><td>★ ★ ★ ★ ★</td></tr>
<tr><td colspan="4">UK</td></tr>
</table>

Player pianos or Pianolas (a trademark name) are demanding companions, needing care and sometimes repair. Ian McLaughlin's website is where to come to find out more.

SPECIAL FEATURES

Below a general introduction is a well-ordered menu under headings such as **How a Player Piano Works**, **History & Development**, **Selection of Music Roll Suppliers**, **Player Piano Societies** and **Books about Player Pianos**. Even though some pages have notes at the bottom explaining that they are 'currently under construction', the material already available is top-class.

Links & Miscellaneous Items takes you to other websites on the same theme, including some overseas.

This is an excellent place in which to start exploration of player pianos – and to find out some intriguing facts along the way.

www.uk-piano.org			
The UK Piano Page			
Overall rating: ★ ★ ★ ★ ★			
Classification: Music		**Readability:**	★ ★ ★ ★ ★
Updating: Regular		**Reliability:**	★ ★ ★ ★ ★
Navigation: ★ ★ ★ ★ ★		**Speed:**	★ ★ ★ ★ ★
UK			

www.moremusic.co.uk			
More Music			
Overall rating: ★ ★ ★ ★			
Classification: Music		**Readability:**	★ ★ ★ ★
Updating: Regular		**Reliability:**	★ ★ ★ ★
Navigation: ★ ★ ★		**Speed:**	★ ★ ★ ★
UK			

Pianos, tuners, restorers, removers, teachers – they are all here, and a lot more besides.

SPECIAL FEATURES

Piano History is a delightful link, leading to a series of articles chronologically arranged in terms of the history of piano development. One is a letter from Beethoven to the piano manufacturer Broadwood, thanking him in most elaborate terms for a new instrument he has just received. Under **Piano Construction** you will find a link headed **FAQ**, and under this again an article about **Purchasing a Second-Hand Piano**. Not only does the whole site operate very rapidly, it is great fun to explore.

Everything you ever wanted to know about pianos, beautifully presented. If only all websites were like this!

More Music may be chiefly a directory of record dealers, but it is some directory!

SPECIAL FEATURES

Finding your way around this website is confusing. From the homepage, the area of the website that is most useful in information terms is found by two methods: First, select **Site Map**, then **Links** under Non Commercial Pages and then select Full Index. Alternatively, shortcut to this point by using a longer URL, **www.moremusic.co.uk/links/default.htm**, and start searching this excellent page. Finding Rare Records Online is one very useful feature of this website.

Try also **Main Resource Page**, under Other Collector Resources, which contains details of Auction Houses, Specialist Collectors' Forums (including a link to **Recordmaster.com**, a free valuation service), Online Price Guides and Collectors' Magazines.

This award-winning website is not the quickest to explore because the routes around it are complicated and overlapping, but it still has to come top of the list for vinyl record collectors.

OTHER SITES OF INTEREST

Piano Studio

www.pianostudio.cc/collantq.html

Lola McIntyre, a piano teacher in central Indiana, has one page here about the pleasures of collecting music antiques, along with some tips. Suggestions like including opera glasses, tuning forks and metronomes in your collection are imaginative by the standards of most other websites in the field.

The Musical Box Society of Great Britain

www.mbsgb.org.uk

The Musical Box Society of Great Britain has lists of **Auctions**, **Museums**, **Suppliers** and **Restorers**. The most useful part of the website for information, though, comes under **Links**.

Roger Gross Ltd

www.rgrossmusicautograph.com

If there is a UK equivalent of Roger Gross, he or she hasn't popped up in the process of researching this book. Roger Gross Ltd, in New York, deals in classical music/opera autographs and memorabilia. The homepage lists the four most recent catalogues, with links in the right-hand box opposite each, to Composers, Conductors, Opera and so on, with occasional special or topical features.

David Robinson

http://privatewww.essex.ac.uk/~djmrob/phono.html

David Robinson is a researcher at Essex University who has had a lifelong love of old gramophones, phonographs and records. In this one page he summarises his collecting interests and gives some useful warnings about fakes.

Old Crank

www.oldcrank.com

Detailed, clearly illustrated examples of what to look out for in fake phonographs (crap-o-phones) are available here from **Articles**. Despite the USA location, there are some good features under **Links** too.

Classical LPs

www.classical-lps.co.uk

This is where to find out about classical LPs issued from the 1950s to 1970s. **Collector's Guide** gives some help with the identification of labels, genuine or otherwise.

B'Side the C'Side

www.bside.freeserve.co.uk

B'Side The C'Side deals in vinyl records. There is so much stuff for sale here, from **African** to **Trad Jazz** and from **Classical** to **Rockabilly**, that it would be a good way of working out either what the value is of the records you already possess, or what you should start to collect.

Rockmine

www.rockmine.music.co.uk

Certainly a website in which to go digging, Rockmine has information on all the great names of Rock, with The Beatles top of the list.

Acoustic Forum

www.acousticforum.co.uk

Acoustic instruments have certainly moved into the collectable category, even if they can hardly yet be classed as antiques. This website is very young and needs to build but may be a good starting point.

photography

Photographs and early photographic equipment form very much a growing area for collectors. This, of course, is a collecting field where even the earliest examples of the art only date back to the mid-nineteenth century. Early examples of photography, like the daguerrotypes detailed below, have been highly prized by collectors for some time, especially where they are of identified people, places or events. But more recently the equipment used in photography has become very collectable too, so that a Victorian stereoscopic viewer or even a modest Box Brownie camera can command a good price, as will be seen from a look at the photographic 'bible', McKeown's Price Guide to Antique & Classic Cameras. In this instance, rarity is more important than actual age. Another field for the collector, of course, is the work of contemporary photographers.

www.daguerre.org
The Daguerrian Society

Overall rating: ★ ★ ★ ★ ★			
Classification:	Photography	Readability:	★ ★ ★ ★ ★
Updating:	Regular	Reliability:	★ ★ ★ ★ ★
Navigation:	★ ★ ★ ★ ★	Speed:	★ ★ ★ ★ ★

US

This website is information-packed, covering everything from the history and development of the daguerrotype process to the now highly collectable product.

SPECIAL FEATURES

Texts leads to a list of nearly a hundred articles, divided under a dozen headings. There are many joys here, including, under **Reminiscences**, an entertaining account by M.P. Simons of how he unexpectedly managed to get 'An Exquisite Picture' of a cantankerous small child. Other features accessed from the homepage include **A Bibliography** and **A Thumbnail History of the Daguerrotype**, reminding us that the process was launched on the world as early as 1839.

Further features investigate the process and the manufacture of daguerrian supplies, while anecdotes from various sources are numerous. The main index ends with **Links**, all exceptionally relevant, and finally **Current News** and **Upcoming Events**. Even then, you have not quite exhausted the riches of this website, for you can still go to **What's New** and explore via the bar that comes at the bottom of each page and on the left of the homepage.

It would be hard to see how this website could in any way be improved.

www.image-gallery.co.uk/collectorsguide.html
Image Gallery

Overall rating: ★ ★ ★ ★			
Classification:	Photography	**Readability:**	★ ★ ★ ★ ★
Updating:	Regular	**Reliability:**	★ ★ ★ ★
Navigation:	★ ★ ★ ★	**Speed:**	★ ★ ★ ★

UK

The Image Gallery specialises in the sale of vintage, fine art and contemporary photographs, but it purveys some useful information too.

SPECIAL FEATURES

It is worth looking at two particular links here. The first is **Collector's Guide**, which gives some useful tips about what to look out for in photograph collecting, especially the identifying marks that prove authenticity. The second is **Vintage Collection**, where clicking on any of the individual examples shown will lead to a larger image and a good description (along with details of price, whihc is helpful in terms of indicating what to collect).

Links, at the time of writing, went only to two sources, the **Royal Photographic Society** (which may be holding exhibitions of interest to collectors), and the **Daguerrian Society** (see previous entry).

Rare photographs, especially in early forms such as daguerrotypes, command very considerable prices these days and this website would help any collector be aware of the main features that make images valuable.

OTHER SITES OF INTEREST

Park Photographic Services
www.parkphoto.co.uk
Here, under the link headed **Collectors' Notes**, you will find some very useful advice for would-be collectors. See also the **Technical Notes** link, which addresses the question of the deterioration of photographs. **Useful Links** will also reward a little exploration.

Bristol – Early Photography
www.brisray.co.uk/bristol/bphoto.htm
Here there is a most informative long article about the importance of the town of Bristol in terms of early photography, inspired by a request from America to identify an early daguerrotype. The article is especially interesting in the account it gives of the research process, and it ends with a good list of links to photography and cinematography websites. These include a feature on **Ensign Cameras** and thence to **The Camera Collecting Ring**, as well as an article about fashion as displayed in cartes de visite.

Museum of the History of Science
www.mhs.ox.ac.uk/cameras/index.htm
Here you will find full details of an exhibition entitled The Technology of Photographic Imaging, held at the Museum of the History of Science in Oxford in 1997. The entire collection can be viewed online, along with a survey of the camera collection under **Overview**, and a study of Early Photographic Images. Two additional features are **Miss Acland & Early Colour Photography in Oxford** and **Lawrence of Arabia & his Cameras**.

Box Cameras
www.boxcameras.com
Paul Barone is an American collector and enthusiast with a good website (despite some very small print) dedicated to 'the history, science and marketing of photography, 1880-1930.'

Antique and Classic Camera Home
http://members.aol.com/dcolucci/index.html
The best website for looking at actual examples of vintage cameras, with numerous relevant onward links.

British Journal of Photography
www.bjphoto.co.uk
The online presence of The British Journal of Photography, this mainly studies the contemporary world of photography, but the **100 yearrs of photos** link, found in the left-of-homepage index, is worth reading. Articles include **Collecting**, **Photojournalism** and **Hobby Photography**.

porcelain & ceramics

This field of collecting, covering everything from the most primitive earthenware to the most sophisticated fine china, is one of the largest. Certainly, you will find that ceramics fills more pages in any Miller's Collectables Price Guide than any other collecting interest, and even in the larger Antiques Price Guides it is only outdone by furniture. It is plentiful, of course, given that a typical family might own perhaps one table and a dozen chairs but many pieces of crockery. Its real charm, however, lies in its incredible variety. Both in form and decoration the choice is virtually limitless and there will surely be something to suit every taste.

---

want to read **more reviews** on this subject?

log on to

www.thegoodwebguide.co.uk

---

www.martra.co.uk
The Susie Cooper Information Site

Overall rating: ★ ★ ★ ★ ★			
Classification: Ceramics		**Readability:**	★ ★ ★ ★ ★
Updating: Regular		**Reliability:**	★ ★ ★ ★ ★
Navigation: ★ ★ ★ ★		**Speed:**	★ ★ ★ ★ ★

(UK)

Although the designs of Susie Cooper are the main focus here, there is more than enough other material about other ceramics designers to warrant a main entry in this guide.

SPECIAL FEATURES

Gallery is where you can view Susie Cooper designs arranged chronologically, showing very clearly the evolution from an obviously Art Deco starting point to a more assured personal style. **Biography** tells her life story, while **Resources** looks at designs she produced for various different manufacturers. In **Archives** there are several interesting articles, one of them being about recent Mabel Lucie Attwell fakes. **Links** is particularly valuable, as it studies the work of several other designers besides Susie Cooper, such as Clarice Cliff and Keith Murray. Loading of all pages is gratifyingly rapid.

This tribute website may seem almost reverential at times but it still covers a lot of ground and is a good introduction to 20th century ceramics designers.

www.tile-collector.co.uk/art-noo.htm
Tile Collector

Overall rating: ★ ★ ★ ★ ★			
Classification: Ceramics		**Readability:**	★ ★ ★ ★ ★
Updating: Regular		**Reliability:**	★ ★ ★ ★
Navigation: ★ ★ ★ ★ ★		**Speed:**	★ ★ ★ ★ ★

(UK)

Jake Ellis has created here a wonderful exposition of what does, and does not, count as Art Nouveau style as displayed in ceramic tiles.

The images throughout this website are stunning, in quality, variety and speed of loading – but the text is well worth reading too. Jake's own comments, made while giving tile designs percentage ratings, are both entertaining and revealing. Basically, there is everything here you could possibly wish to know.

SPECIAL FEATURES

Go to the bottom of the homepage for an excellent list of links to further pages, set against a lilac background. This is so well laid out that no further explanation of how to use it is needed here. Suffice it to say that the section headings are **Tile Condition, Factories & Styles, Tile Identification, Collecting Tiles, Factory Faults** and **Other Info**. At the very bottom of the page is a link to Jake's other website, **Tile Heaven**, where you can view tiles for possible purchase. Here, image-loading is much slower but, again, there is plenty of information in support, all of it well written and relevant.

Okay, it's only about tiles, but what a lot of marvellous information there is here!.

www.griffinpeers.freeserve.co.uk
In Search of Georgian China - Antique China Web

Overall rating: ★ ★ ★ ★			
Classification: Ceramics		**Readability:**	★ ★ ★ ★
Updating: Regular		**Reliability:**	★ ★ ★ ★
Navigation: ★ ★ ★		**Speed:**	★ ★ ★

UK

Gaile M. Griffin Peers, editor of online magazine **Antiques Review** (links from this website) also has this website about Georgian china.

SPECIAL FEATURES

Access the site by clicking on the link headed **Georgian China – The Book**. You are then offered pages starting with **Introduction** and **Background**, and then progressing through **Shapes, Porcelain Marks, Patterns** and so on. Unfortunately you will find that you have to use the back button each time to return to the list and pick up the next page, which makes progress slow. Having worked through this part of the website you now need to return to **Front Page**.

Picture Gallery shows a good selection of china in blue and white, Imari Style and Famille Rose. Clicking on any of the thumbnail illustrations will enlarge it and probably offer several different views of each piece. **Links** offers a list of some predictability but may still be of use.

Despite its slightly odd layout, this website is still worth your time if 18th and early 19th century china is your collecting interest.

www.antiques-and-arts.com
Antiques and Arts

Overall rating: ★ ★ ★			
Classification: Ceramics		**Readability:**	★ ★ ★
Updating: Regular		**Reliability:**	★ ★ ★ ★
Navigation: ★ ★		**Speed:**	★ ★ ★

UK US

This website is directed at the collector of antique (especially English) ceramics and porcelain.

SPECIAL FEATURES

You have to click on the red 'Antiques and Arts Home' link to reach the homepage which, on a background of little Kate Greenaway girls, has a most insistent (even irritating) flashing question mark, headed **Star Buy?** Clicking on that produces the same frenetic question mark, multiplied, and a third click transports you to the item in question. There seems no justification for the four-question-mark stage, given that all four boxes lead to the same illustration – a case of somewhat over-excited web designer-itis (purveyed in this case by Stef Zelynskyj). Don't let it put you off, though, because there are good things in this website too. **FAQ** is a good place from which to start exploring, especially as the answers explain the UK connection.

Multiple images of pottery and china for sale form the distracting background to each page, and further superimposed images flash from all directions. Many links transport you only to the email contacts of the dealers who contribute to the site. This would allow you to notify them of a particular collecting interest, admittedly, though it may be a little disappointing not to see more online details of items for sale. Further areas of the website are going live soon, however.

Art Deco Pottery is one area of the website where individual items, many of real quality (and considerable price), can be viewed online. Pictures are exceptionally good and load well, though the automatic opening of new windows – which then need to be enlarged and subsequently closed – is confusing at first. **Antiques Newsletter** contains some extreme examples of the jokey-jargon style of web-writing, so avoid it if you think it's going to annoy you. Similarly 'more contemporary British art from a.k.a. british artist' is found in **Hamilton B. Gallery**, including a video installation proposed for the Old Royal Baths at Bath, called Dreams Curiosity and Drowning Video, which your system may not be powerful enough to support.

This is eccentric, flashy and confusing for the first-time visitor, hence the navigation star-rating above, but if you are a real antique ceramics and porcelain enthusiast you will find it worth persisting.

OTHER SITES OF INTEREST

Stockspring Antiques – Antique English Porcelain
www.antique-porcelain.co.uk
Stockspring Antiques in Kensington Church Street, London, is a specialist dealer in fine antique English porcelain. The website is full of beautiful images under such topics as **18th and 19th Century Porcelain**, **English Porcelain Figures** and **Decorative Porcelain**. For further illustrations, see the record of the exhibition, **The Dragon and the Quail**, featuring English Kakiemon Porcelain, which Stockspring held in February to March 2000.

Porcelain: Marks
www.users.skynet.be/rutrene/marks.html
This is a most interesting feature about the widespread practice of faking porcelain marks throughout the 18th and 19th centuries.

The Clarice Cliff Collectors Club
www.claricecliff.com
The Clarice Cliff Collectors Club website demonstrates that the incredible current popularity of Clarice Cliff's designs continues unabated. It allows you to explore her life and her designs, and warns about fakes.

Koh's Antique Ceramics Corner
www.fortunecity.com/victorian/song/270/antiquecorner.htm
This Singapore-based website is devoted to Chinese ceramics, with numerous links and a wealth of information on such topics as Ming or collecting blue and white china.

Gotheborg.com
www.gotheborg.com
This should be of help to anyone seeking to identify Chinese 20th century marks, an elaborate matter, hence the fact that, as the website owner says, it loads 'like a dead duck.' Be patient, because it does work. To confuse you even further, there is a feature on **Chinese Marks on Japanese Porcelain! Factory Marks** and **Artists' Names** are also linked. **Chronology**, incidentally, looks at the history of China the country rather than china the product.

Logoi.com
www.logoi.com/notes/reignmarks.html
There is a little more help here towards identifying the marks on Chinese porcelain.

PorcelainSite.com – Porcelain Marks
www.porcelainsite.com/porcelain/marks/start.shtml
This focuses on Thuringian china, though it contains some more general historical information too.

Abbey Ceramics Encyclopaedia
www.abbey-ceramics.co.uk
This may well develop into one to watch in future, depending on whether it manages to fulfil its avowed intention of making the Abbey Ceramics Encyclopaedia the most

important point of reference on the web for ceramics enthusiasts. So far the only individually detailed manufacturer is Doulton but others are to be added soon.

Note: Finally, here are two websites that have relevance for collectors of glass as well as those interested in porcelain and ceramics:

Bedford Borough Council
www.bedford.gov.uk
Bedford Borough Council has a feature within its website about the Cecil Higgins Gallery. Higgins was a passionate collector of ceramics and glass. There are two good introductory articles here, found by clicking on **Out and About**, then on **Tourist Information Centre** and selecting 'C' from the alphabetical index to find the Cecil Higgins Art Gallery link. The two articles in question are under **Ceramics** and **Glass** in the blue links across the top of the page.

Reference Works
www.referenceworks.co.uk
Reference Works are sellers of books on the topic of ceramics, some of which are probably difficult to find elsewhere. The catalogue is listed down the left-hand side of the homepage, and does in fact also cover **Glass & Other Decorative Arts**. Under the **Geoffrey Godden** link is information about this well-known expert's books and periodic talks on the subject.

postcards

Postcards can be worth anything from a pound or two to a hundred pounds or more, all depending on what they depict. Topographical cards, showing identified places, are always a good bet, as are those showing known historic figures or events. There are many other categories in which the collector can specialise, from the glamour photographs of stars of the stage and, later, the screen, to the unselfconsciously vulgar cards sold to seaside holidaymakers. To make sense of postcard collecting, and to understand what makes a card valuable, you may find the following websites to be of use. Online information about postcards is scarce but even by viewing the pages of a few dealers, whose names you would find by a standard search, you would learn a lot.

www.postcard.co.uk
Postcard Pages

Overall rating: ★ ★ ★ ★			
Classification:	Postcards	**Readability:**	★ ★ ★ ★ ★
Updating:	Regular	**Reliability:**	★ ★ ★ ★
Navigation:	★ ★ ★ ★ ★	**Speed:**	★ ★ ★ ★ ★

UK

This comprehensive website introduces the whole business of postcard collecting, only second to stamp collecting in popularity.

SPECIAL FEATURES

Start by clicking on **Collecting** and you are offered a list of two dozen onward links, including an introduction to the hobby, details of **National Postcard Week**, UK and worldwide postcard clubs and a feature entitled **What Are Postcards Worth?** It turns out that postcards of local railway stations pre-1950 are dramatically more valuable than those of any other subject.

Other links include **News**, **Fairs** and **Printers & Publishers**. The Links area of this website is extensive too, with good lists under dealers in the UK and worldwide, and **Collectors & Clubs**.

This has to be the best starting point for any collector of postcards.

OTHER SITES OF INTEREST

The Flea Market

www.the-flea-market.co.uk/postcards

There are two very short articles here that may be of use, one on Caring for Postcards and the other headed Glossary & Abbreviations.

Dave's Cave

www.davecave.org.uk

Included not quite as a joke, this is the way postcard collecting is presumably going to go! Dave's Cave will enable you to send – and collect – what are already known as ecards.

posters & advertisements

Not far removed, perhaps, from ephemera (see pp.78ff), posters and advertisements have often been extremely decorative and striking. They are very collectable, partly because relatively few survive in good condition. The range of websites listed below is mainly restricted to British, American or European posters but if your interests lie further afield, don't be put off. Posters from other countries will be found perfectly easily through a good search engine. Try the words 'early posters' in Google's search facility, for example, and you will be offered Egyptian, Russian, Chinese, Nazi and many other posters, including early music and film posters.

www.internationalposter.com
International Poster Gallery

Overall rating: ★ ★ ★ ★ ★			
Classification:	Posters	**Readability:**	★ ★ ★ ★ ★
Updating:	very regular	**Reliability:**	★ ★ ★ ★
Navigation:	★ ★ ★ ★	**Speed:**	★ ★ ★ ★ ★

US

Here you will find a fine catalogue, with particular strengths in Italian, Swiss and Soviet posters, along with a really valuable introduction to the subject as a whole.

SPECIAL FEATURES

The excellent article about early posters and poster collecting is found in the very small print at the bottom of the homepage, under **Intro to Posters**. Also most informative is the article **A Key to Poster Value**. This lays out very clearly the factors that enhance a poster's value, as well as those that reduce it, such as fading, folding or dry-mounting.

About Us is another interesting feature, explaining the history of the Gallery, which is in Boston, Massachusetts. It was opened in 1994 by Jim Lapides, a collector and private dealer who is now, via the internet, bringing his passion for posters to a global public. **Poster of the Day** features an individual poster from the collection, along with a brief article. **Books** leads to an excellent list, probably the most comprehensive you will find, and helpfully sorted under nationalities or headings such as War and Propaganda, Art Nouveau, Art Deco, Travel and so on.

For good, solid information about posters from all corners of the world, this is where to start – a really professional and elegant website.

www.idesirevintageposters.com
I Desire Vintage Posters

Overall rating: ★ ★ ★ ★			
Classification: Posters		**Readability:**	★ ★ ★
Updating: Regular		**Reliability:**	★ ★ ★
Navigation: ★ ★ ★ ★		**Speed:**	★ ★ ★ ★

(CAN)

The shop opened in Toronto over ten years ago, but Valerie and Jim Clark are now using the internet as the means of bringing their collection of vintage posters to a wider audience.

SPECIAL FEATURES

The illustrations, all in colour, are sometimes rather faded in their on-screen presentation, no doubt in the interests of rapid loading. The various areas of the site are accessed via the lilac bar below the homepage header. **Vintage Posters** and **Collecting Vintage Posters** are the most informative areas, while **Gallery** is the place in which to browse or purchase. This last link divides the posters into categories, which are listed down the left-hand side of the page. Clicking on the thumbnail picture of any item will lead to a larger, clearer illustration, a price (in dollars) and a red button whereby to make an email enquiry.

In a field where informative material is scarce, this otherwise commercial website is better than most.

OTHER SITES OF INTEREST

Antique Maps and Prints
www.antiquemapsandprints.com
This site has a section on old advertisements, and also hosts www.postaprint.co.uk, which is a good source of early advertising material for sale. Prices are quoted in dollars.

Poster Group
www.postergroup.com
Mickey Ross, an American businessman in the textile industry, made a hobby of collecting old posters in the free time he had when travelling. Gallery displays the wonderful collection he has amassed, while Store takes you to the shopping facility within the site. An excellent range of posters but with no background information.

Chisholm Larsson Gallery – Vintage Posters
www.chisholm-poster.com
Another enticing US-based hunting ground, with a vast selection, including posters from many different countries, from the two World Wars, and on many different topics, from travel to theatre and cinema.

Poster Shop
www.postershop.co.uk
Worth a look, particularly if you are thinking in terms of buying and would rather pay sterling prices.

A to Zee
http://atozee.com/books/art/posters.shtml
A good list of books about posters and advertisements, with onward links to Amazon.

Henniker – Old Advertisements
www.henniker.org.uk/html/old_ads.htm
Part of the website of Dave Henniker, one of whose interests is **Old Advertisements**. His collection is displayed on two pages of thumbnail photos. Clicking on any image will enlarge it, but there is no additional information.

radio, tv & sound recording

There is no shortage of websites about old radios but most are either dealers in radios and radio parts, or they are offering online displays of old wireless models. To enter this collecting field you almost certainly need a degree of technical expertise, as restoring and repairing radios and televisions is skilled work. The following websites offer good information for collectors and, especially, restorers:

www.bl.uk/collections/sound-archive
National Sound Archive

Overall rating: ★ ★ ★ ★ ★			
Classification:	Sound	Readability:	★ ★ ★ ★
Updating:	Regular	Reliability:	★ ★ ★ ★ ★
Navigation:	★ ★ ★ ★ ★	Speed:	★ ★ ★ ★ ★

UK

The National Sound Archive is part of the British Library and the catalogue is massive, with nearly 2.5 million recordings.

From the homepage the links are not immediately visible. Move the cursor over 'Collections', 'Services' and 'Information', however, and various options will appear. Using the Information route first, a little arrow will pop up directing you to the left of the photograph, where live links will now come up for the first time. **About Us** is one such link, which is a good starting point.

SPECIAL FEATURES

Research is probably going to be the area of most interest to collectors. Having opened this page, scroll down to the oval buttons and click on **Artefacts** to find details of the Archive's gramophone and phonograph collection, as well as an explanation of other things it does not contain, such as radios or televisions.

Now, returning to the Resources page, you will find other useful features from the oval buttons, such as **Record Labels** and **Websites**. From within the latter is a good feature on the **History of Sound Recording**.

This information-rich website lives up to the standards one would expect of the British Library's National Sound Archive.

www.valve.demon.co.uk
Vintage Radios UK

Overall rating: ★ ★ ★ ★ ★			
Classification:	Sound	**Readability:**	★ ★ ★ ★ ★
Updating:	Regular	**Reliability:**	★ ★ ★ ★ ★
Navigation:	★ ★ ★ ★	**Speed:**	★ ★ ★ ★

(UK)

Malcolm Bennett originally trained as a 'Sparks' (radio operator) in the Merchant Navy, which led to a career in the commercial sector with various major companies. His website is large, informative and generally well organised.

SPECIAL FEATURES

Here you can buy or get repaired more or less any sort of radio. Recently, by customer demand, **Wanted** and **For Sale** sections have also been introduced. These are so popular that they will soon need sorting into categories. You can also find out a great deal about the history and development of radios from the radio button alongside **Links to On-line Displays, Collections** and **Personal Pages in the UK and Europe**. Meanwhile **Resources, Books and Magazines** includes information about four periodicals for radio enthusiasts as well as a good list of books.

The professionalism of Malcolm Bennett is evident throughout this website. The overall scope of the site is what earns it a major entry here.

www.penders.cwc.net/otindex.html
The Old Tellys Site

Overall rating: ★ ★ ★ ★			
Classification:	TV	**Readability:**	★ ★ ★ ★
Updating:	Regular	**Reliability:**	★ ★ ★ ★
Navigation:	★ ★ ★ ★	**Speed:**	★ ★ ★ ★

(UK)

Whereas restoration advice about old radios is plentiful, Steve Pendlebury's website is one of very few for televisions.

SPECIAL FEATURES

Most of the information here is addressed to those who already have quite a bit of basic knowledge of electronics. Assuming that level of expertise, this is certainly the place to look for specific TV-restoration advice. Links include such things as **Power Supplies, Sound Problems, Monochrome Tubes** and the like, leavened with the occasional lighter topic such as **Wives Survival** (contributed by Steve's wife, Dilys Taylor). If you still need more information of a practical nature, try **Essential Reading** for a helpful booklist.

Old Tellys Forum is the discussion area of the website, and **Boring Page** tells you a little about Steve himself. Finally **Links & Webring** gives you a good list of other websites to look at and ends with the now famous 'Worst of the Web' winner, **Pylon of the Month**.

As television styles change, older models begin to look more and more 'antique' and this is therefore bound to become a growing field for collectors. There aren't many websites to help the would-be collector yet, though – but this is as good a starting point as you are likely to find.

OTHER SITES OF INTEREST

Past Times Radio

www.pasttimesradio.co.uk

Past Times Radio is mainly concerned with selling vintage radios or offering a restoration service. Under **Recent Restoration Projects**, however, are such detailed descriptions of the restoration processes involved that any radio enthusiast could learn a great deal. Other links include a **Vintage Radio Events Calendar. Links and Suppliers** leads to a page not easy to read given the combination of print colour and background, but the websites listed could well prove useful.

Vintage Radio

www.vintage-radio.com

Paul Stenning's website concentrates on the repair of vintage radios and is extremely information-rich, with an excellent list of sub-topics appearing as you click on each item in the left-margin index. **Recent Repairs** lists about thirty different models, each of which is both illustrated and described in great detail. The **Links** list here is outstanding.

The British Vintage Wireless Society

www.bvws.org.uk

The British Vintage Wireless Society's website is limited in online interest but it does list the contents of recent issues of the journal **BVWS Bulletin** and also provides a calendar of forthcoming events.

Mikey's Vintage TV Page

www.oldtechnology.net

Mikey's Vintage TV Page is practical and well organised, despite some very small print to sub-links. The main index is in the left of page margin, where you need to scroll down through the cartoon-style picture boxes to get at all the areas of the website, even including Marmaduke the cat. Mikey's interests extend to old video recorders, tape recorders and gramophones as well as one player piano.

scientific instruments

This section begins with two websites for collectors of medical instruments, followed by two concerned with scales and weights, and then a website devoted to more general scientific instruments. With only a couple of exceptions, all the websites in this section are American, including the subsequent shorter entries. This illustrates the strength of US-based collecting in this field, certainly, but it is perhaps disappointing, in that it also indicates the absence of equivalently good UK-based sites. The American slant would matter less if it were true that scientific and medical instruments were universal on both sides of the Atlantic, but unfortunately this is not always the case. Collectors will find the following websites of general use and interest, therefore, but may find them somewhat frustrating too.

www.antiquescientifica.com
Alex Peck Medical Antiques

Overall rating: ★ ★ ★ ★			
Classification:	Medical	Readability:	★ ★ ★ ★ ★
Updating:	Regular	Reliability:	★ ★ ★ ★
Navigation:	★ ★ ★	Speed:	★ ★ ★ ★ ★
US			

Alex Peck is a collector in Charleston, USA, fascinated by the medical history of the American Civil War.

Be warned that the homepage is very long, and you won't discover everything unless you scroll right down to the bottom of the screen.

SPECIAL FEATURES

Archives is a well-illustrated guide to items in the Peck collection, but **Articles** contains only one feature. Below the heading **Actively Buying Medical Antiques** is a long list of all the items Mr Peck is interested in acquiring. Below this is the section **Medical Antiques Introduction Series** which is still under development – only those items that are underlined are 'live' links.

Collecting Alerts is a most interesting feature, illustrating a large number of fake items, several of which look worryingly authentic to the untrained eye. Finally, the website also features reference books and a commercial area.

This website is larger and more interesting than perhaps it at first appears, with only the American emphasis depriving it of a five-star score. Needless to say, a few items are not for the squeamish.

www.medicalantiques.com
Medical Antiques

Overall rating: ★ ★ ★ ★			
Classification:	Medical	Readability:	★ ★ ★ ★
Updating:	Regular	Reliability:	★ ★ ★ ★
Navigation:	★ ★ ★ ★	Speed:	★ ★ ★ ★
US			

As it says, 'the internet resource for collecting medical, surgical, apothecary, dental and bloodletting antiques.'

SPECIAL FEATURES

Click at the bottom of the homepage where it says **Enter: Medical Antiques Collecting**. You now have a long index in view, divided under Private Collection Photos & Information, Articles about Medical and Dental Antiques; Dealer, Collector, Seller and Advertising services; Books, Data and References; and Links to Museums and Medical Antique Websites.

Articles are mostly both long and detailed. A good starting point for the new collector would be **How to Get Started Collecting Medical Antiques**. Onward links are numerous and relevant.

This is probably the best website from which to start researching the field of medical antiques.

http://home.clara.net/brianp/index.html
English Weights and Measures

Overall rating: ★ ★ ★ ★			
Classification: Scales/Weights		**Readability:**	★ ★ ★ ★
Updating: Occasional		**Reliability:**	★ ★ ★ ★
Navigation: ★ ★ ★ ★		**Speed:**	★ ★ ★ ★

UK

www.scales-and-weights.com
Scales & Weights

Overall rating: ★ ★ ★ ★			
Classification: Scales/Weights		**Readability:**	★ ★ ★ ★
Updating: Regular		**Reliability:**	★ ★ ★ ★
Navigation: ★ ★ ★ ★		**Speed:**	★ ★ ★ ★

US

The possible abandonment of the English weights and measures system, evolved over a millennium, causes anguish in some quarters. The details of the present system are laid out here in great detail, with some good information for collectors.

SPECIAL FEATURES

Collecting Weights explains that collectors are more interested in commercial (marked) weights than those for domestic use. **Names on Weights** will be of great use to any collector wishing to identify the various companies who were authorised to make weights, and the dates at which they were active. **Picture Gallery** presents thumbnail shots of weights, which you click to enlarge. Pictures of coins follow.

History is a very rudimentary chronological table. Other pages are dedicated to different measures, such as those for **Lengths & Areas**. There is also a link to **ISASC**, the International Society of Antique Scale Collectors, a single page with information about the Society, and a membership application form. **Anti-Metrication** expands on the view that abandoning the present British weights and measures system is both unnecessary and wrong.

Here there is practical information, probably of most use for identifying those companies who manufactured weights and measures.

Though USA-located, this website is clearly not written by a native English speaker, but it is nevertheless well constructed and very useful. Note that if you want to return to an earlier page, using the Back button at the top of your screen will only move what appears in the central section of your screen. You will need to use the Back command at the top of the menu if you wish to return to the original options.

SPECIAL FEATURES

Clicking on Enter, you now have to select a scales type from a short menu on the left of the page, either **Antiquity**, **Opium**, **Coin**, **Commercial**, **Pharmacy** or **Letter**. Your choice may produce a secondary menu, subdividing the scales types again, but eventually you will be offered a selection of illustrations in the right-hand margin, from which you scroll down to select whichever is nearest to your particular query. You now need to use the internal scroll bar to the left of this margin to view the enlarged image in full, along with its description below.

Links, found at the extreme right of the header bar, is very well worth your time. The actual connections are in the pictures alongside each website description.

A good website with plenty of information and excellent links.

www.antique-scientific-instruments.de/antique.html			
Instruments of Science and Technology			
Overall rating: ★ ★ ★			
Classification: Science		**Readability:**	★ ★ ★
Updating: Occasional		**Reliability:**	★ ★ ★ ★
Navigation: ★ ★ ★ ★		**Speed:**	★ ★ ★ ★
ⓅⓄ			

This is the private collection of Peter W.H. Kirschbaum; a very impressive collection indeed.

SPECIAL FEATURES

Click first on **To the Collection**. You will now see a three column page, with an object illustrated centrally, an enlargement of that same object to the right, and the main index to the left. Selecting any item from the index will bring up another picture or pictures in the central column, which you can then enlarge at will. Picture quality is excellent even if descriptions are minimal. Occasionally, there is more information available but unless you can read German you will need to download the online translator before you can make use of it.

Interesting Links are divided under two headings, **To Museums** and **To Private Collections**, but although the former is quite a substantial list the latter contains only one item, which is disappointing.

The usefulness of this website is in the illustrations rather than any descriptive material (hence the modest star-rating above) but it certainly demonstrates what a really top-class collection of scientific instruments might contain.

OTHER SITES OF INTEREST

Scientific and Antique
www.antiquescience.com
The most useful part of this website for the collector will be the Links, divided under six headings: **Microscopy**; **Medicine**; **Mathematical**; **Physics, Mechanics and Electronics**; **Astronomy** and **Museums and Miscellaneous**. Though the headings that then come up are brightly legible, the descriptions of what each link contains are hard to read (red lettering on a black background) but try not to be put off, as this is a rich hunting ground.

365 Publications Ltd – Echoes in Time
www.365publications.co.uk/Magazine/Article6.htm
Here you will find a long, well written and well illustrated article entitled 'Collecting Medical and Surgical Antiques' by Douglas Arbittier, MD, an American enthusiast.

The Gemmary
www.gemmary.com
The Gemmary, in California, specialises in Antique Scientific Instruments and Old and Rare Books. **Other Interesting Websites** is where you will find the onward links that may prove most useful. **F-Files: Fakes Forgeries Frauds** is interesting but as yet limited.

Scientific and Medical Antiques
www.utmem.edu/~thjones/sci_ant.htm
Scientific and Medical Antiques, although yet another American page, offers such good and extensive links that this resource should not be ignored. Exploring the history and development of scientific instruments is a strength here.

sewing items

Even the smallest home might have room for a collection of sewing items. These charming relics of domestic life are very often exquisitely made, partly because sewing, embroidering and doing tapestry-work (as opposed to mending) have tended to be the preserve of the wealthy, leisured classes. Having made that observation, there seems to be no website specifically dedicated to the study of small, conveniently collectable sewing items. At the less convenient end of the scale, indeed at the downright heavy end, are sewing machines, and here the internet has more to offer, as the following websites show. Otherwise, collectors should investigate the larger gateway websites listed at the beginning of this Guide.

www.treadles.com
Alan Quinn's Treadles.com

Overall rating: ★ ★ ★ ★ ★			
Classification: Sewing		**Readability:**	★ ★ ★ ★ ★
Updating: Occasional		**Reliability:**	★ ★ ★ ★ ★
Navigation: ★ ★ ★ ★		**Speed:**	★ ★ ★ ★

UK

Sewing machines were once objects of great beauty, not merely practicality, and Alan Quinn truly appreciates them.

The homepage here is a long one and it is worth scrolling right the way down, because the seven link buttons across the top of the page, although duplicated below, are presented with no explanation.

SPECIAL FEATURES

First come a few special features added to the website no more recently than January 2000; then explanations of the half dozen different types of sewing machine shuttle and, after that, lists of sewing machine makes, divided by English and German manufacturers. Below this again you will find American manufacturers (all Singer models are listed here, though actually made in the UK, US and Canada), Swiss, Canadian and Japanese makers.

Links to Online Sewing Machine Manuals comes next, followed by a feature on the **Care and Restoration of Machines**, which should be of great use to any collector. Finally **Recommended Sites** leads to a quite remarkable list of relevant websites, their national origin indicated by little flags.

No other sewing machine website will give you as much information as this.

OTHER SITES OF INTEREST

International Sewing Machine Collectors' Society
www.ismacs.net/home.shtml
This is the International Sewing Machine Collectors' Society, based in the USA. The website is as yet fairly new and is still developing but may be worth watching.

Button Images
www.buttonimages.com
Button Images is dedicated to the preservation of button art. **Buttons** is the link to online sales, while **Collector Info** has items on cleaning buttons, and on their Identification in terms of what materials have been used in their manufacture. Once again, this is an American website, so the **Other Links** are mainly to American dealers or enthusiasts.

silver

Silver dealers on the internet are very numerous and many have very attractive websites, but very few of these offer any background information beyond the details of items for sale. The one area that is reasonably well addressed online is hallmarking, and with a certain amount of persistence you should now find it possible to identify hallmarks using the online resources listed here. What you will probably not find is any very satisfactory historical material about the evolution of silver designs or about the most famous silversmiths. As a really professional website would actually be a good vehicle for illustrating the design differences that characterise, say, Georgian or Regency silver, this is a pity. Meanwhile, you will have to pick up what you can from viewing the wares of online dealers.

www.bryandouglas.co.uk
Bryan Douglas Antique Silver

Overall rating: ★ ★ ★ ★			
Classification:	Silver	Readability:	★ ★ ★ ★
Updating:	Regular	Reliability:	★ ★ ★ ★ ★
Navigation:	★ ★ ★ ★ ★	Speed:	★ ★ ★ ★

UK

Bryan Douglas, one of the foremost London silver dealers, has a smart, efficient website here. It is mainly a shop window, of course, but there is some background information too.

SPECIAL FEATURES

For the collector wanting to know more about silver, this website offers two especially useful areas. One is under the link **History**, which, although it is chiefly a history of the London Silver Vaults, also explains the unique hallmarking system used in Britain for some six hundred years. The other is **Smithing**, which explains the tools and techniques used by silversmiths over the ages.

Inventory lists all the items currently for sale, illustrated with thumbnail black and white photographs that can be enlarged by clicking. Because the range is so large, this in itself forms a good resource.

There is limited information about the history or techniques of silversmithing here, but what there is would certainly act as a good introduction to the topic.

OTHER SITES OF INTEREST

Daniel Bexfield Antiques
www.bexfield.co.uk
Daniel Bexfield in London's Burlington Arcade has an elegant website, with a **Features** link that leads to four articles on silver and related subjects. There is also a very comprehensive online display of items for sale.

BBC Online – Housecall
www.bbc.co.uk/homes/housecall/antiques.shtml
Click on Silver, under Household and Other Everyday Objects, and a short article full of advice will appear in a new window.

Christopher A Long – Silver Collection
www.christopherlong.co.uk/print.silcol.html
Single article about the recently re-discovered silver collection at the Ritz Hotel in London, with some very good advice for collectors.

British Hallmarks
www.bhi.co.uk/hints/hmarks.htm
& www.bhi.co.uk/hints/hmarks2.htm
These two pages are found within the British Horological Institute's website (see p.70). They are much the best for explaining the hallmarking system concisely and yet in practical detail. The first covers London, Birmingham and Chester; the second Sheffield, Glasgow and Edinburgh.

British Hallmarks
www.click4gold.co.uk/british_hallmarks.htm
Another introduction to British hallmarks is found here, on a single page with only one onward link, right at the bottom, to the **Hallmark Database** within the Collectiques website (see p.16). From this, select **Decode Hallmarks** and then work progressively through the identification process.

smoking items

Smoking pipes, using snuff certainly, and even smoking cigarettes are all pursuits that are increasingly unfashionable. In the past, of course, things were very different and an elegant cigar-holder, a quaintly carved pipe or a silver cigarette case was very much an item of fashion. No wonder, therefore, that such objects are now very desirable. Moreover, it seems that the sort of people who collect smoking items, whether at this level or at the somewhat less expensive cigarette packet, card and paper level, are also the sort of people who put the details of their hobby on the internet. As a result, there are several good, informative websites available for anyone interested in this collecting field.

www.pipe-smokers.co.uk
Pipe and Pouch

Overall rating: ★ ★ ★ ★ ★			
Classification:	Smoking items	Readability:	★ ★ ★ ★ ★
Updating:	Regular	Reliability:	★ ★ ★ ★ ★
Navigation:	★ ★ ★ ★	Speed:	★ ★ ★ ★ ★

UK

Pipe and Pouch is a serious website dedicated to 'the noble art' of pipe smoking and places little Sherlock Holmes silhouettes as links on its homepage. There are links to shops, but the emphasis is on information.

SPECIAL FEATURES

You will find plenty of historical and cultural information, especially in the area entitled **Yesteryear**. On the homepage there is an overview of the history of smoking in England, a **History of the Pipe**, a feature on Alfred Dunhill and an article entitled **First Light**, about the inventor of the safety match, John Walker. **Snippets** and **As It Was** offer further fascinating nuggets of background information.

Help & Answers offers two invaluable instruction pages, **How to Pack & Light a Pipe** and **Which Lighter**. **Questions & Answers** addresses such problems as **Burn Out**, **Gurgling Pipe** and **Strange Taste**. For even more information, try **Pipes** which includes **Caring for Pipes**, or **Tobacco**, where there are four features about tobacco types and blends.

Directory Links are mainly to commercial websites and located in **Pipe & Pouch Hot Links**. Confusingly, **Links** is an opportunity to add your own link.

There is good entertainment as well as plenty of hard factual information to enjoy here, whether or not you are a smoker.

www.wclynx.com/burntofferings/index.html			
Jim's Burnt Offerings			
Overall rating: ★ ★ ★ ★ ★			
Classification: Smoking Items		**Readability:**	★ ★ ★ ★ ★
Updating: Regular		**Reliability:**	★ ★ ★ ★ ★
Navigation: ★ ★ ★ ★ ★		**Speed:**	★ ★ ★ ★
US			

James A Shaw has put together an extremely stylish and informative website, certainly one of the best on this topic.

SPECIAL FEATURES

Investigate this website from the links below the central picture. These include **Boxes & Tins**, **1880s Trade Cards** and **A Pretty Face** (examples of advertising using pictures of women). **International Smokes** takes you to China between the Wars but, from links below, also to a host of other countries, England among them. You will find, in fact, that many pages have such additional links at the bottom. Moreover every page throughout this website is presented with a short, literate introduction.

Nicotiana Recomendi leads to an exceptionally good and detailed list of other website links, leading to nearly forty websites where the emphasis is more on information than on dealing.

The wealth of illustrations here makes some pages a little slow to load but be patient – you will unquestionably find it worthwhile.

http://home.online.no/~smpeders/index.htm			
Svein Martin's Home Page			
Overall rating: ★ ★ ★ ★			
Classification: Smoking Items		**Readability:**	★ ★ ★ ★
Updating: Regular		**Reliability:**	★ ★ ★ ★
Navigation: ★ ★ ★ ★		**Speed:**	★ ★ ★ ★
NOR			

Svein Martin Pedersen introduces himself as 'a man with many hobbies and a dangerous collecting habit'. The hobbies are mainly musical – Blues, Cajun, Country & Western, Rockabilly – and the collection is **Cigarette Packets**.

Unless you want to explore the music area of the website, don't click either the flashing box that says 'Enter' or the **Main Page** link below. Instead, scroll down the page through the introduction to the collection. Below this, and below the flags and subsequent list of all the countries represented in the collection, is a series of links to all the other areas of the website. This method of exploring is easier for the first-time visitor than using the grey buttons down the left-margin index, as there is more explanation.

SPECIAL FEATURES

You can now investigate the most pictorially rewarding area of the website, with features like **The Posters Galore**, an extensive article on **Cuba – Cigarette Lithographs**, another on **Egyptian Samples** and another on **Rare Cigarette Cards**. Note, incidentally, that **This Month's Selected Packet** is a richer source than it may appear, because there is a button at the bottom of the page via which you can view all the packets featured in this display since the website was launched in January 1996.

Right at the bottom of the list are the onward links, under **Cigarette Pack Collectors** and also, in fact, under **Julia's Page**, as this is the webpage of Julia Carlson, an Australian collector. You will find that clicking on the highlighted names in the list of collectors will only bring up email contacts. You need to use the little green arrow boxes to be transferred to their websites.

Throughout this website there is, understandably, quite an emphasis on the Norwegian aspects of cigarette packet collecting, but because it ranges worldwide also it is genuinely useful to collectors anywhere, including the UK.

OTHER SITES OF INTEREST

Elizabeth Smoking
www.jannoo.dircon.co.uk/kentwell/library/misc/smoking. html
Here there is a single page about smoking in Elizabethan times, a pursuit as controversial then as it is now!

Clay Tobacco Pipes
www.dawnmist.demon.co.uk/pipdex.htm
Clay Tobacco Pipes is the name of this website and the passion of Heather Coleman who, with her partner Natalie (a terminally ill, painfully articulate woman, whose battle with anorexia is recounted in detail as a warning and help to other sufferers), designs and makes clay pipes for present-day pipe-smoking enthusiasts, costume productions and the like. Importantly, though, there is good historical information about clay pipes here too. Work down this page and you will find a very large index, studying pipes from 1600 to 1930, all divided by design and date.

Snuffs and Snuff Taking
www.snuffbox.freeserve.co.uk
Snuffs and Snuff Taking claims to be the only non-commercial snuff site, and is actually very informative. The homepage offers **Why this Web Site? What is Snuff?** and **How to Take Snuff**, among other items. Somewhat more whimsical are **Fribourg & Treyer, of Blessed Memory** (purveyors of snuff) and **Chagall's Pinch of Snuff** (a painting). Links include **Snuff Bottles & History of Snuff in China**.

The Tobacconist
www.the-tobacconist.co.uk
Largely a commercial website, The Tobacconist nevertheless has a little information that may be of use to collectors. Try Collectables, even though at the time of writing there was only one item featured, and Hot Links, where there are a few other websites you may like to view.

Legacy's Tobacco Silks
http://home.paceball.net/zdenek/01tabacco.htm
Legacy's Tobacco Silks are divided into two displays, American and British, and both exquisite collections can be viewed online here.

The Arcadia Bell Collection
http://web.ukonline.co.uk/arcadia.bell/Home.htm
The Arcadia Bell Collection of cigarette papers is well illustrated here. Exploration is merely a matter of using the links at the bottom of the homepage. The absence of any recent postings in the Update Log suggests that this website may no longer be being actively maintained.

Cartophilic Society of Great Britain
www.cardclubs.ndirect.co.uk
CSGB is the Cartophilic Society of Great Britain, a source for cigarette card enthusiasts as well as for collectors of other types of card. Once again, it is probably the Links section of the site that will be of greatest use to collectors.

sports memorabilia

The trade in sporting memorabilia is enormous, with the emphasis being massively in favour of football, ahead of any other sport. Cricket holds its own in this world, however, and there is a distinct difference between the two. The collectors of football memorabilia are being offered, via Ebay and similar auction websites, relics of a very contemporary nature indeed, such as programmes autographed by players still actively engaged in the game. Cricketing memorabilia appears to need a longer pedigree before it becomes really collectable. Rugby, golf, tennis and athletics put in minor appearances and some sports, like rowing, are apparently of no interest to collectors at all.

www.sports-photographs.co.uk
Sporting Heroes

Overall rating: ★ ★ ★ ★			
Classification: Sports		**Readability:**	★ ★ ★ ★ ★
Updating: Regular		**Reliability:**	★ ★ ★ ★
Navigation: ★ ★ ★ ★		**Speed:**	★ ★ ★ ★

UK

www.knights.co.uk
Knight's Sporting Memorabilia Auctions

Overall rating: ★ ★ ★			
Classification: Sports		**Readability:**	★ ★
Updating: Regular		**Reliability:**	★ ★ ★ ★
Navigation: ★ ★ ★		**Speed:**	★ ★ ★

UK

Photographer George Herringshaw came up with the idea of posting at least one image of the great sports stars of the last 30 or more years, for posterity. It is a non-commercial site.

SPECIAL FEATURES

About Us explains the object of this website in more detail, including the policy about downloading images (permissible for personal use). The potted biographies that accompany the photographs are contributed by volunteers, and more are needed. **Charity Information** details the six charities that sponsor the website.

The sports represented are **Athletics, Cricket, Football, Golf, Rugby** and **Tennis**, and the photographs are all action shots of high quality. This website is still actively being developed.

As a reference base this already has value but it should develop into something even more useful as it builds up.

Knight's hold quarterly auctions of sporting memorabilia at Leicester County Cricket Club, and the homepage lists both recent and forthcoming auctions. All areas of the website are open, including **Results**, and no subscription is required.

SPECIAL FEATURES

There is usually a link, in blue in the centre of the page, to highlights of recent auctions. Otherwise you need to search via the index in the left-of-homepage margin. At first glance, it appears extremely rudimentary, with only **Home Pages**, **Cricket Memorabilia**, **Sporting Memorabilia** and **Results** as options, but as soon as you click on any of these further drop-down menus appear.

Cricket tends to be where the main emphasis lies, with football in second place, though the balance of the list will change all the time, of course, as auctions come and go. Bidding can be done by post, fax, email or telephone and, of course, in person.

This auction house has good lists and a perfectly practical website.

OTHER SITES OF INTEREST

Sporting Memorabilia
www.sportingmem.co.uk
Sporting Memorabilia is a purely commercial website with the emphasis heavily in favour of football. As a source for collectors wishing to identify values of such items, it is useful.

CrickInfo
www-uk.cricket.org
CrickInfo has some historical material listed under the heading Database in the index. Links here include **Pictures**, **Statistics**, **Grounds** and **Archive**. The list under **Links** is excellent, if you can be bothered to wait for it.

The Cricket Memorabilia Society
www-uk4.cricket.org
The Cricket Memorabilia Society invites your membership here and solicits views about all sorts of issues in the cricket world. Its overall object is to promote the appreciation and care of cricketing memorabilia.

Cricket Lore
www.cricketlore.com
Cricket Lore magazine covers both historical and contemporary issues in cricket. Its website is simple, encouraging you to subscribe and offering about three online articles you can read as examples of its output.

Programme Monthly & Football Collectable
www.pfmc.co.uk
Programme Monthly & Football Collectable has a straightforward website, with an index on the left of the homepage that includes **Collecting as a Hobby** and **Collector's Club**. **Black List** should be read before entering into any deals. **News** is also interesting, currently containing a feature about fake World Cup 1966 programmes.

The Splendid Whizzer Association
www.splendidwhizzers.com
Finally, this is one for lovers of motor-sport. Articulate, quirky and amusing, The Splendid Whizzer Association admits to prejudice in its choice of what vehicles (land, sea or airborne) to feature. There is good historical material here, including an article about Brooklands past and present under **Features**, and another about the Land Speed Record under **L.S.R.** There are also good lists under both **Events** and **Links**.

stamps

Stamp collecting has long been extremely popular and several major collections have recently fetched very serious sums of money at auction. Indeed, even some individual stamps, especially what the non-expert might consider simply 'wrong 'uns' (stamps that got printed incorrectly or were only part-perforated) can be worth amazing sums. At the beginner level, though, anyone at all can enjoy this interest. Being young or less than well-funded is no bar to becoming a collector of stamps. Website owners have recognised this and, as a result, this is the only area of antiques or collectables on the internet that has websites specifically directed at children. The first entry in this section is such a site, but it is so good that any novice collector may as well start here.

www.1840on.co.uk
1840on Stamp Collecting

Overall rating: ★ ★ ★ ★ ★			
Classification:	Stamps	Readability:	★ ★ ★ ★ ★
Updating:	Regularly	Reliability:	★ ★ ★ ★ ★
Navigation:	★ ★ ★ ★ ★	Speed:	★ ★ ★ ★ ★

UK

The URL of this website won't let you forget the date of the first Penny Black – and enthusiasts have been collecting the relics of postal history ever since. This website is admittedly aimed at a young readership, but it is so clear that any new collector would benefit from reading it.

SPECIAL FEATURES

The options available from the homepage are explained in the horizontal bars. They include **Do You Want to Know More About Stamp Collecting?** and **Information for All Stamp Collectors**.

Collecting News & Articles includes two features on British First Day Covers, one on Thematic Collecting and another about George VI Stamp Collecting. Other areas accessible from the homepage include **Collecting Shows & Fairs,** and links to dealers.

In the middle of the page is Links to Other Sites for Collectors, Societies/Clubs/Trade/etc. These include **Coin and Banknote Collecting Sites** and **Railway and Railroad Societies & Clubs**.

Don't dismiss this website just because it is aimed at younger or beginner collectors. It's well put together, clear and user-friendly, and a good starting point for any stamp collector beginning to explore the internet as a resource.

www.ukphilately.org.uk			
UK Philately			
Overall rating: ★ ★ ★ ★ ★			
Classification: Stamps		**Readability:**	★ ★ ★ ★ ★
Updating: Occasional		**Reliability:**	★ ★ ★ ★ ★
Navigation: ★ ★ ★ ★ ★		**Speed:**	★ ★ ★ ★ ★
UK			

This is the best reference point for the adult collector.

SPECIAL FEATURES

Introducing Philately is the best place to start, with a handy reference list down the right-hand side of the page explaining all the different areas open to the collector. **Where to See Stamps** not only introduces the major collections but also gives details of opening times, admission charges and telephone contact numbers.

Find a Society for me enables you to consult a UK map to see where all local, national and specialist philatelic societies are located. Most can at present only be contacted by snail-mail or telephone. **What's On** is a list of events, though updating is erratic. **Buy and Sell Stamps** is advisory rather than a link to a list of dealers. Other items in the main index are self-explanatory. The last three items, however, need explanation as only their initials are given. **ABPS** is the Association of British Philatelic Societies and is well worth exploring, especially for the onward links; **BPT** is the British Philatelic Trust, an educational charity for the promotion of philatelic studies; and **NPS** is the National Philatelic Society.

Clear and eminently readable, this is a basic resource for all stamp collectors.

www.royalmail.com			
Royal Mail			
Overall rating: ★ ★ ★			
Classification: Stamps		**Readability:**	★ ★ ★
Updating: Regular		**Reliability:**	★ ★ ★ ★ ★
Navigation: ★ ★ ★		**Speed:**	★ ★
UK			

The Royal Mail has an area of its website dedicated to collecting, found under **Stamps and collectibles** in the left-of-homepage index. It is, however, aimed at children. Movement around the site is remarkably slow.

SPECIAL FEATURES

Using the link above, you will be offered a drop-down menu starting with **Stamps 2001 Collection**. In the same menu, **Originals Catalogue** leads to details of a new set of collectable items created to celebrate three hundred years of the Royal Mail, and **The Poetry of Stamps** is a feature celebrating the same occasion.

Previous Stamp Issues only go back to 1997. To enter the **Young Collectors** area of the website you need to give a name and email address (a fictional one will get you in if you don't want to receive emails). This is aimed at very junior collectors using a treasure-hunt approach.

This is a very disappointing effort considering the huge riches the Royal Mail surely could put on the web.

OTHER SITES OF INTEREST

The Royal Mail and Telegraph Group
www.telegraph.co.uk/ads/r/royalmail/philhome.html

This is a joint feature between The Royal Mail and Telegraph Group newspapers. It is merely a gateway to nearly twenty articles but among them there are some real nuggets. They include **How Air Letters Came to Take Off, Forgotten Treasures from a Lifetime Ago** and **When Queen Victoria was left with egg all over her face**.

Stamps.co.uk
www.stamps.co.uk

Stamps.co.uk is an online resource for stamp collectors, with an area for **Beginners** (the same page as the Telegraph and Royal Mail collaboration above), a **Discussions** forum, some up-to-date **News** and a very detailed but mainly commercial **Links** list.

The Great Britain Philatelic Society
www.gbps.org.uk

The Great Britain Philatelic Society is not the same as the National Philatelic Society or the Royal Philatelic Society (see below). Its emphasis is more on events and participation, as well as producing a **Journal** and a **Newsletter**, housing a **Library** and publishing **Books**.

The Royal Philatelic Society
www.rpsl.org.uk

The Royal Philatelic Society, London, has a very straightforward, attractive website. The **Links** section is good. Otherwise its website its mainly a route to finding out what is held in its own library collections, which would tell you whether a visit would be worthwhile.

The Association of Great Britain First Day Cover Collectors
www.gbfdc.co.uk

The Association of Great Britain First Day Cover Collectors has a good, clear website, with an area for **Young Collectors**, as well as an **Events** link listing the GBFDC's own events, details of the **Magazine**, 'First Day Coverage' (not readable online), and occasional **Special Offers**.

Stampworld
www.stampworld.co.uk

Stampworld, based in Cardiff, claims to list websites under **Philatelic Links** that do not appear elsewhere. Some, certainly, are not familiar from other websites. Its main object is stamp dealing, however.

Stampex
www.stampex.ltd.uk

Stampex is a regularly held stamp-collecting event at the Business Design Centre in Islington, London. Dates are given here, plus a little other practical information.

textiles & soft furnishings

Textiles, here, is a bit of a catch-all term for what has turned out to be a list of websites devoted mainly to two areas, patchwork quilts and lace. It is, of course, not at all surprising to find that the best quilting websites are American. The making of patchwork quilts, in an extraordinary variety of imaginative designs and colour-combinations, has long been a strength of American needlewomen, especially in the southern States and, for instance, in the Amish community. Lace, on the other hand, has very strong English and European roots. This difference in the location of the two skills is very clearly reflected in the 'nationality' of the websites.

http://mail.kosmickitty.com/MainQuiltingPageS.html			
World Wide Quilting Page			
Overall rating: ★ ★ ★ ★ ★			
Classification:	Quilting	**Readability:**	★ ★ ★ ★ ★
Updating:	Regular	**Reliability:**	★ ★ ★ ★ ★
Navigation:	★ ★ ★ ★ ★	**Speed:**	★ ★ ★ ★
US			

Established in 1994, this claims to be the oldest (and best) quilting site on the web – probably true. Downloading illustrations compromises speed a little.

SPECIAL FEATURES

About a third of the way down the homepage you will find the start of the index proper, under Topics on the World Wide Quilting Page. It starts with **How To's**, an introduction to quilting techniques, and **Quilting Terms Glossary**. Quite a bit of practical information follows, and then an area of discussion, message boards and questions. Regional Information includes **Quilt Stores and Guilds**, and this area, as well as **Supplies & Shopping Online,** has a largely though not exclusively American emphasis.

Where things get really interesting is in **Other Places in the Web to Visit** and subsequent links, especially **Quilting History** which heads the list of websites in Quilting Library.

If the serious quilt collector can't find anything of interest here it will be very surprising.

OTHER SITES OF INTEREST

Joachim and Betty Mendes
www.mendes.co.uk

Joachim and Betty Mendes have a shop in Brighton, dealing in antique lace, textiles, fans, costume and other associated items. Although this is effectively their online shop window, there is a lot of useful historical information here too, alongside the descriptions of what is for sale. Note that the index is at the bottom of the page, so you need to scroll down to it.

Artizania & Artfairs
www.artizania.co.uk

Artizania & Artfairs specialise in antique costume and textiles, Artizania being an umbrella for dealers, and Artfairs running regular specialist Fairs in Leeds, Malvern and Manchester. There is also a listing of events worldwide. **Links**, at the bottom of the left-of-page index, lists first UK links, then USA links and, finally, Information Links.

The Lace Guild
www.laceguild.demon.co.uk

The Lace Guild exists to promote lacemaking and to this end it runs events and produces publications, all listed here. The **Craft of Lace** link does give a very brief introduction to the various types of lace.

Lace Making in the 17th Century
www.portsdown.demon.co.uk/lace.htm

This is a single page on lace-making in the 17th century.

Honiton Lace Shop
www.rafis.demon.co.uk/indexlace.html

This is the website of the Honiton Lace Shop, the last remaining lace shop in Honiton itself. It is mainly a commercial site, of course, but there is good information about the history of Honiton lace found from the **Lace Questions?** link.

The Lace and Lacemaking Webring
www.netcentral.co.uk/~geoffana//lacering/index.html

The Lace and Lacemaking Webring Home Page is attractive, with its fine beaded dragon, but not especially clear. To investigate what it has to offer you need to click on **Lace & Lacemaking Webring Index**, which takes you to a directory of all the websites in the ring, currently one hundred.

Tattered
www.geocities.com/Heartland/5082/

Tattered has the goal of making the art of tatting better known worldwide. There is only a little historical information here but the site is quite detailed and densely packed, and should reward exploration.

Workbox Needlecrafts Magazine
www.ebony.co.uk/workbox/backiss.htm

Here you will find a backlist of issues of the magazine 'Workbox.' Although these cannot be read online, the descriptions of the contents of each issue are so detailed that you would easily discover whether there had been an article about your own particular collecting interest.

quilts

Patchwork Quilts – Their Origins and Development
www.llph.co.uk/Patchwork-History.htm

There is a good single page here on the history of patchwork quilts, within what is otherwise the purely commercial website of the Linen, Lace and Patchwork House.

The Quilt Gallery
www.thequiltgallery.com

The Quilt Gallery is a commercial website selling some 1500 quilts at any given time under a number of headings, starting with **American Quilts** and then **Antique Quilts**. The sheer number of quilts displayed here makes it an interesting reference point.

Antique Quilt Source
www.antiquequiltsource.com
This is also an American online source of antique quilts to buy, particularly those from Pennsylvania. Descriptions are good and thorough, making this too a useful historical resource.

Antique Quilts
www.antiquequilts.com
No apologies for listing a third commercial quilt website. This one has two useful links, though neither very detailed, How to Hang a Quilt and How to Wash a Quilt.

American Quilts
www.americanquilts.com
Finally, one more online 'superstore' displaying both contemporary and antique quilts, especially those made in the Amish community.

toys

Toys are, by their very nature, likely to get damaged. Children are seldom careful owners and, in any case, completely unused toys would hardly seem to have served their purpose. This does mean, though, that relatively few toys survive in good condition, and scarcity always leads to high prices – so a really excellent clockwork, tinplate toy from around 1900 can fetch a four-figure sum. On the internet, toys of every conceivable sort are traded, even those that seem to be only a season or two out of date. It would be completely impossible to list them all here, so only a few key websites are given. Always topping the popularity stakes, however, is the same toy, the teddy bear.

In this section, general toy websites come first, followed by a selection of more specialist websites. Dolls come next, and teddy bears last.

want to read **more reviews** on this subject?

log on to

www.thegoodwebguide.co.uk

www.toy-box.com
Toy Box

Overall rating: ★ ★ ★			
Classification: Toys		**Readability:**	★ ★ ★
Updating: Regular		**Reliability:**	★ ★ ★
Navigation: ★ ★ ★ ★		**Speed:**	★ ★ ★

UK

This is a good idea but is as yet very incomplete. The object is to build up really first-rate databases of toys and toy manufacturers to enable collectors to do research on the web. This is the **Encyclopedia** part of the website.

SPECIAL FEATURES

On the occasions visited, the **Auctions** area of the site produced nothing at all for **Collectibles,** which was completely empty, as was the **Adverts** area, so either these are not being much used or they are not being sufficiently publicised. **Bookshop** and **Links,** however, both led to good directories. The list of books in particular seemed impressive and could build into a very useful resource.

A valuable idea has been launched here but a lot more needs to be done if it is to develop into something useful.

OTHER SITES OF INTEREST

Dmoz
http://dmoz.org/Recreation/Collecting/Toys
The Dmoz project has assembled a good list of links to pursue if you are a toy collector, though there is very little available in the **Reference** section at the bottom of the list. It is noticeable that the number of websites available for Teddy Bears is easily the largest.

Kidd's Toys
www.kiddstoys.co.uk
Though a commercial website, Kidd's Toys offers good descriptions and many illustrations. There is also a particular interest in Japanese and German toys.

Hornby-Dublo Electric Trains
www.mollymo.freeserve.co.uk
This is a site dedicated to the collectors of Hornby-Dublo electric trains. Look at **Frequent Hornby Questions** and the Reference Section at the bottom of the homepage for information, or **The Virtual Swapmeet** to deal or exchange.

Batman Memorabilia
www.kelly1.demon.co.uk
Ed Kelly is a Batman enthusiast and under the **About** link he gives an interesting account of how he got into collecting.

The Tri-Ang Society
www.tri-angsociety.co.uk
The website for Tri-ang enthusiasts, with lots of information and good onward links.

Golly Corner
www.my-home.demon.co.uk/golly.htm
The Robertson's golly continues to be unfailingly popular despite assaults by PC-obsessives. Liz Prigg maintains this excellent website.

dolls and teddy bears

Buying dolls, dolls' houses or teddy bears over the internet is not a problem. Finding dedicated websites that help you with advice about what to look for is much more difficult. Much the best advice is found within the general antiques and collecting websites listed earlier in this book, such as the BBC Online – Antiques (see p.15), with articles by both David Dickinson and Hilary Kay, or Antiques World (see p.13), which has an article by Constance King.

http://come.to/afewgoodbears
A Few Good Bears

Overall rating: ★ ★ ★ ★			
Classification:	Toys	**Readability:**	★ ★ ★ ★
Updating:	Occasional	**Reliability:**	★ ★ ★ ★
Navigation:	★ ★ ★	**Speed:**	★ ★ ★

US

To enter this website you need to click on the title in the middle of the page. You will find that your cursor has been hijacked by a little bear face that now accompanies it everywhere, but in fact it still operates normally.

SPECIAL FEATURES

This website is incredibly 'cute' in design, presentation and text, presumably because it is aimed at children, but it does contain some limited practical information. **Once Upon a Bear** gives a brief potted history, while **What's in a Bear** gives advice about selecting a well-made bear. **Bear With Me** is about caring for teddy bears.

If you can cope with the way the information is delivered – and after all, it is really meant for the young – this may be of a little practical use.

have you registered for free updates?

log on to

www.thegoodwebguide.co.uk

OTHER SITES OF INTEREST

Teddy Bears on the Net
www.tbonnet.com

This is the website of Teddy Bears on the Net. It's an appealing website but it is American so, for instance, the only teddy bears shows listed are all in the USA.

Absolutely Bear
www.absolutelybear.ukf.net

Absolutely Bear by Fiona Smith is a cleverly designed and attractive commercial website that is still rapid and user-friendly, and is UK-based. Click on **Enter** in the middle of the homepage and then select the areas of the website you want to visit either from the main page links or from the paw-prints down the left margin. **On the Road** takes you to the list of shows where Fiona and her bears can be seen. **Links** leads to a list of dealers, mostly in the UK but including also a few abroad. The most useful of these for collectors is probably **Bear Artists of Britain**, an impressive list.

Promoting Teddy Bears in the UK
http://teddybearsuk.members.easyspace.com

Finding your way around this website takes some persistence but the way in is via the Union Jack flag, centre-page. From this point on things get simpler. You now need to click on one of the street signs, explanations of which are given in yellow text opposite. The list includes bear artists, repairers, museums, clubs and so on. One of the best is the link to **Magazine**, which turns out to be 'The Tedegraph.' Here at last, although it's all directed at children, you can pick up a little practical information about **Bear Care** and possibly enjoy a look at the **Rare Bears** link.

TeddyUK
www.teddyuk.co.uk

TeddyUK has a much more detailed historical look at the origins of teddy bears than most other teddy bear sites. It is found from the **Other** link, selecting **Teddy Bear History** from the pop-up possibilities.

Sue Pearson Tedd Bears
www.sue-pearson.co.uk

Sue Pearson is an established teddy bear dealer and authority based in Brighton. You can order her book or video here, and enquire about repairs, but the main value of the site is probably in its illustrations.

Yiffle
www.argonet.co.uk/users/lyndale/lotcaf/yiffle/plushies/teddybears

This remarkably long URL might not be worth the effort unless it led, as it does, to the best list of books about teddy bears to be found on the net.

Dolls of the World
www.dollsworld.co.uk

Dolls of the World is a magazine for anyone interested in collecting dolls, of all periods and nationalities. It can't be read online but you can find out what has appeared in recent issues and subscribe.

Virtual Valley Graphics
www.virtualvalley.co.uk

Virtual Valley Graphics has, as only a small part of its website, a feature on collectable dolls, from both today and the recent past. To find it, you need to use the **Enter** button and then select **Doll Showcase** from the bottom of the Index. **Hints 'n' Tips** is well worth a few minutes of your time.

transport memorabilia

This is a collecting field where you really do need to confine yourself to UK-based websites if your interest lies in British-made modes of transport: aircraft, ships, trains and motor cars. This is a case where American websites, except in the case of aircraft, won't do.

This section is arranged in alphabetical order as follows: **Air, Rail, Road, Sea**.

air

Entering the words 'aviation memorabilia' in a good search engine like Google produces some 32,000 results, so sifting out the best is no easy matter. The majority, however, are American – some are very good, like the first few listed here – and for that reason they may be of limited interest to all but the most avid UK-based collectors. Adding 'UK' to the search criteria will reduce the number of hits to not much above a thousand.

One of the frustrations of using the internet is that websites are often not removed as promptly as they should be – or, sometimes, not removed at all – when they are out of date. For instance, at the time of writing, the auction of the important Flayderman Collection was being advertised by Butterfields. The only problem was that it had happened in November 2000 and this was now four months later.

---

www.leisuregalleries.com
Leisure Galleries

Overall rating: ★ ★ ★ ★ ★			
Classification:	Aviation	**Readability:**	★ ★ ★ ★
Updating:	Regular	**Reliability:**	★ ★ ★ ★
Navigation:	★ ★ ★ ★ ★	**Speed:**	★ ★ ★ ★ ★

(US)

Leisure Galleries is an American website dealing in aviation memorabilia, militaria and related autographs.

SPECIAL FEATURES

The left-of-homepage index offers various items of **Aviation Art,** mainly by British artists Robert Taylor and Nicolas Trudgian, as well as **Luftwaffe Signed Photos** (Luftwaffe being a speciality of the Gallery), **German Medals and Decorations**, **Signed Books**, **American Aces' Signed Photographs** and the like. At the time of writing, **Commemorative** ('Commerative' on the homepage, unfortunately) **Envelopes** included one by Arthur 'Bomber' Harris and another by Douglas Bader, among others.

About Leisure Galleries offers photographs of the Gallery's owners and a brief introduction, including the information that the Gallery has been in existence since 1984 and welcomes international orders with payment by credit card. Contact is by email, phone or fax, though an illustrated catalogue can be ordered online from the **Order Our Color Catalog** link.

An attractively presented website bound to appeal to true aviation enthusiasts.

www.aviation-antiques.com
Aviation Antiques

Overall rating: ★ ★ ★ ★			
Classification:	Aviation	**Readability:**	★ ★ ★ ★ ★
Updating:	Regular	**Reliability:**	★ ★ ★ ★
Navigation:	★ ★ ★	**Speed:**	★ ★ ★

US

Jon Wm. Aldrich in California (part of whose email address, rather charmingly, is 'oldjon') deals in aviation memorabilia.

SPECIAL FEATURES

The collection is divided into four dated periods between 1900 and 1955, and in each case sub-divided into Military and Civilian. Everything is well described and extremely well illustrated, which is what earns this otherwise purely commercial website an entry here. Items range from books, instruction manuals and photographs to actual fittings and fixtures from historic planes and pilots' medals. Purchasing involves making contact by telephone. Sadly, there is no information available from the website about Jon himself, nor are any onward links available (hence only four stars above). All we glean is that he is himself a retired pilot. No matter, perhaps; the website he runs is clear and efficient.

If you're prepared to pay dollars and import duty for anything you buy, this could prove useful. Simply viewing this website would still be informative, though.

OTHER SITES OF INTEREST

Aeroflight
www.aeroflight.co.uk
Aeroflight calls itself 'The Website for Aviation Enthusiasts', which is not a bad description. It's not aimed especially at collectors but the information in this site is considerable and the **Media** link from the homepage may well be worth exploring, as well as details of forthcoming **Airshows**, at the bottom of the index.

Historic Flying
www.historic-flying.com/index.htm
Only come to Historic Flying if you are really a big-league collector. Not long ago on this website you could only buy either a Brewster F2A-1 Buffalo or a Griffon Hovercraft!

rail

On the whole, this Guide does not list Museum collections, partly because it would then become little more than a list of Museums and could not possibly be comprehensive. Occasionally, however, there seems to be no other option, and certainly, when it comes to the study of railway history and what is rather cumbersomely known as 'railwayana', the National Railway Museum in York has to be the first port of call, both on and off line. Considering how popular this is as a collecting interest, it is surprising perhaps that there are not more websites on this topic. Such sites as can be found are listed next.

www.nrm.org.uk				
National Railway Museum				
Overall rating: ★ ★ ★ ★ ★				
Classification:	Railways		**Readability:**	★ ★ ★ ★ ★
Updating:	Regular		**Reliability:**	★ ★ ★ ★ ★
Navigation:	★ ★ ★ ★ ★		**Speed:**	★ ★ ★ ★ ★
UK				

Railway history, advertisements and posters, books and periodicals, photographs and paintings – they are all here at the National Railway Museum in York.

SPECIAL FEATURES

Probably the best place to start is **Billboard,** which explains the layout of the website. **Exhiblets** features small, online digital exhibitions. One of these featured **Railway Posters** and two others revealed parts of the Museum's great photographic archive.

At the bottom of the **Research & Archives** page is an online enquiry form, where a member of the museum staff will try to reply within five working days to requests for information. This is a free service, though those wishing to do in-depth research are encouraged to visit and do the work themselves.

Other areas of the website, such as **Visiting, Commercial Services** and **What's On** are self explanatory. Incidentally, **Links** only connects to a list of commercial organisations. A more useful list, from the point of view of the researcher, is found at the bottom of the Research & Archives page, under **Other Sources of Information & Research**.

An unfussy, five-star starting point for anyone wanting to explore railway history and memorabilia.

www.d444.freeserve.co.uk/Webring/home.html				
Railwayana Webring				
Overall rating: ★ ★ ★ ★				
Classification:	Railways		**Readability:**	★ ★ ★ ★
Updating:	Regular		**Reliability:**	★ ★ ★ ★
Navigation:	★ ★ ★		**Speed:**	★ ★ ★
UK				

Andrew Watts is the 'webmaster' here, managing a large website that will be enjoyed by railway enthusiasts. Note that it features exclusively British railways.

SPECIAL FEATURES

The links are available only from the left-of-page menu, not from the list on the main area of the homepage. This menu is headed by **Auctions & Events,** offering a map of the British Isles with tiny red dots indicating event locations. If this is difficult to use, simply use the scroll bar on the right of the newly superimposed window, and this will enable you to review the entire list. Other items in the menu are straightforward, though certain gaps in information will show up as the site is explored.

Very much a website for and by railway 'buffs', there is nevertheless a lot of good, accessible information here.

OTHER SITES OF INTEREST

Railwayana
www.railwayana.com
Robin J. Gibbons maintains a stylishly constructed website, which contains a special feature on China's Railways. Otherwise it is what he calls 'mainly UK-centric', giving details of a number of recent and forthcoming auctions as well as a list of specialist auctioneers.

Railway Collectors Events Diary
http://website.lineone.net/~tony.hillman/diary.html
Tony Hillman offers a very good list of railwayana auctions, nationwide, with onward links to some of the auctioneers' own websites.

Within the Antiques World website (see p.13), there is a useful feature on **Railway Ephemera** by Robert Forsythe.

1840 on Stamp Collecting
www.1840on.co.uk
Finally, even though it is directed at children, and focused on stamp collecting (see p.127) there is a link available from the homepage to Railway and Railroad Societies and Clubs.

road

The early days of 'motoring', a term which now seems rather charmingly old-fashioned, have a romance all their own. The memorabilia of that era are certainly very collectable now, starting with the cars themselves and including all their various fittings, and even the clothes that were worn by their drivers. Plenty of such items are traded online but yet again there seems to be something of a dearth of practical information or advice for collectors.

www.vccofgb.co.uk
Veteran Car Club of Great Britain

Overall rating: ★ ★ ★ ★			
Classification:	Cars	**Readability:**	★ ★ ★ ★ ★
Updating:	Regular	**Reliability:**	★ ★ ★ ★ ★
Navigation:	★ ★ ★ ★ ★	**Speed:**	★ ★ ★ ★

UK

The Veteran Car Club of Great Britain has its online presence here, and membership is invited. It is the oldest British Society dedicated to the preservation of veteran and Edwardian motor vehicles.

SPECIAL FEATURES

Apart from those elements of this easily used website that are self-evident, **Links** is probably the area most worthwhile for the collector to explore. First, though, take a moment to enjoy the ten cars displayed in the **Gallery,** and the two little 'movies' below (you need the appropriate software for the latter). You can also move from the bottom of the homepage index to details about the **London to Brighton Run**.

From **Links** now investigate further, especially under **Clubs, Museums or non-commercial sites**. Note that you need to click accurately on the green buttons to move forward. One of these is to the **Vintage Sports Car Club**, another equally good source and one that offers further good lists under its own **Links**.

If you are a lover of the early days of motoring you will find that plenty of enjoyable time can be spent here.

OTHER SITES OF INTEREST

Wheels
www.wheels.co.uk

Wheels is a website for bus enthusiasts, notably those who love the Midland Red, and in the real world it has a shop selling bus models and a restaurant in a railway carriage. Online, it offers quite a bit of historical information about buses, accessed from **Introduction**, **What is Midland Red?** and **Preservabus**. This last link explains the involvement in bus restoration projects.

See also **Splendid Whizzers Association** on p.126.

sea

Nautical memorabilia as a collecting field proved surprisingly intractable. The internet did not by any means come up with numerous good resources for those wanting to find out about British ships, let alone for those who might want advice about what to collect from the great days of seafaring.

www.cutter.swinternet.co.uk/home.htm
Maritime History and Sailing Cutters

Overall rating: ★ ★ ★ ★			
Classification: Ships		**Readability:**	★ ★ ★ ★
Updating: Occasional		**Reliability:**	★ ★ ★ ★
Navigation: ★ ★ ★ ★ ★		**Speed:**	★ ★ ★ ★

UK

The owner of this website, Kevin Olsen, has put together a lot of historical information about early sailing cutters (seventeenth to nineteenth century). It is well-organised and very interesting material for anyone researching the background to this period of British sailing ships.

SPECIAL FEATURES

Among the articles available from the homepage is one on **Thomas Shepheard, Cutter builder** and another entitled **Who Were the 18th Century Smugglers?** Meanwhile an article on Catamarans makes the startling revelation that there was a catamaran sailing in English waters as early as 1663.

Particularly interesting is the link to the **UK Sailing Index**, available from the bottom of the page, which leads to a list from which you can then select **Maritime History**. Clicking here gives you access to over twenty further websites that will expand your historical knowledge.

This is a wonderful way in which to learn more about maritime history, if not specifically about collecting nautical memorabilia.

OTHER SITES OF INTEREST

Ships of the Old Navy
www.cronab.demon.co.uk/INTRO.htm
Michael Philips has posted here a great deal of historical information under the title Ships of the Old Navy. The links from the left-hand margin index are arranged alphabetically by ship name.

Clicksmart
www.clicksmart.co.uk/Boats.htm
The Clicksmart directory, launched in September 1999, lists information resources for various subjects, in this case boats and ships. It is worth trawling through the long list of links to see if there is anything of relevance to your own researches.

Clipper Maritime Antiques
www.maritime-antiques.co.uk
Robin Langford of St Ives, in Cornwall, has put two pages on the web here illustrating some of the items in his collection of maritime antiques. The photographs can be enlarged by clicking but no written descriptions are given to support them.

Kaleden.com
www.kaleden.com/cats/2118-3-12392.html
Within this large American collecting/dealing portal, you will find that this price guide to nautical memorabilia is interesting for the range of items illustrated. Practical information is scanty, however.

wine

This is a big collecting field but before you start there is an issue here that is applicable to all collectors of antiques, but especially to the collector of fine wines – are you collecting wines to drink yourself in due course, or as an investment? Your approach will be governed according to your answer to that question.

Sotheby's and Christie's (see p.34 & p.35) both conduct regular wine-related auctions.

Don't forget, by the way, that if wine in general is one of your principal interests you should obtain a copy of **The Good Web Guide to Wine** by Tom Canavan.

www.binclub.co.uk			
The Bin Club			
Overall rating: ★ ★ ★ ★ ★			
Classification:	Wine	**Readability:**	★ ★ ★ ★ ★
Updating:	Regular	**Reliability:**	★ ★ ★ ★
Navigation:	★ ★ ★ ★ ★	**Speed:**	★ ★ ★ ★ ★
UK			

The Bin Club has grown from an idea launched in 1977 by Jim Hood, Chairman of Howells of Bristol Ltd, who saw that serious wine collectors needed storage facilities in the UK for times when they were abroad. It is now located in Wickwar, Gloucestershire.

Few homepages load as quickly as this one, and hardly any are as delectable! The Bin Club now has not far off two thousand members in seventy-five countries around the world.

SPECIAL FEATURES

Flavours of the Bin Club and **How it Works** are the two links that explain the scheme, along with the details under **Further Information**.

Wine Offers are made twice yearly to members, the wines selected being suitable for storage and yet starting from as little as £5 per bottle. **Membership** (£30 initially and then a monthly amount – £50 suggested as a minimum) and **Joining Us** take you into the scheme.

This is a really useful service for collectors, either those abroad or those without convenient storage facilities.

www.bath.ac.uk/~su3ws/wine-faq/			
The Internet Guide to Wine			
Overall rating: ★ ★ ★ ★			
Classification:	Wine	**Readability:**	★ ★ ★ ★ ★
Updating:	Occasional	**Reliability:**	★ ★ ★ ★ ★
Navigation:	★ ★ ★ ★ ★	**Speed:**	★ ★ ★ ★ ★
UK			

Brad and Dri Brown, living in Southern California, have posted this wonderful website about wine on the net. Here in the UK it is hosted by Bath University. It is worth looking at its USA-located website too, as there is some additional information there.

SPECIAL FEATURES

Introduction is the place to start. This is a self-confessed 'wordy' website because, as the compilers say, it is designed to 'provide content, not demonstrate all the fancy bells and whistles a browser can muster.'

Consult the **Table of Contents** for a quick overview of the vast extent of this fascinating website. It offers everything from an explanation of **Phylloxera vastatrix** to recipes for a **Pan-Galactic Gargle Blaster**. The **Index** link helpfully rearranges all the features in the Table of Contents into alphabetical order, a convenient shortcut for future visits.

Among other delights there is an amusing article de-mystifying the rituals and pretentiousness of drinking wine in certain establishments.

Just about everything you ever wanted to know about wine is here and, what's more, it's written in an entertaining manner. Great fun.

www.wineontheweb.co.uk
Wine on the Web

Overall rating: ★ ★ ★ ★

Classification:	Wine	Readability:	★ ★ ★
Updating:	Regular	Reliability:	★ ★ ★ ★ ★
Navigation:	★ ★ ★ ★ ★	Speed:	★ ★ ★ ★

UK

This is a totally independent online wine magazine, edited by wine expert Andrew Jones. Some pages load somewhat slowly.

SPECIAL FEATURES

The homepage gives brief explanations of the items, which are also accessible from the left-hand index. What is novel here is the awareness of the ways in which new technology can be of use to oenophiles, as you will see from consulting the **Radio Postcard** or the **Handheld User** links.

Unusually, there is a special area of the site devoted to **Whiskies & Beers**, while **Consumer Advice** includes articles on **Starting a Cellar** and **Decanting to Breathe**. Other elements are **Vintage Charts, Features** (interesting articles), **Wine Clubs, Books** and **Useful Wine Sites.** This last feature will certainly prove worth exploring as the list of links is well chosen, even though the majority of websites selected are American.

This is a good source of information about wines for all collectors, whether wishing to drink their wines or to store them for investment purposes.

OTHER SITES OF INTEREST

The Fine Art of Wine Collecting
www.365publications.co.uk/Magazine/Article1.htm
Here, you can read an article by George Heritier entitled The Fine Art of Wine Collecting. At the bottom of the page is a link to the punningly-named Gang of Pour website, a North American website with plenty of entertaining articles.

Christopher Keiller Fine Wine Services
www.gladys.demon.co.uk/finewineservices.html
This is the website of Christopher Keiller Fine Wine Services. Scroll down the page to find **A General Guide to Wine Investment** and several other links. **Special Features and Tasting Notes** leads to an article assessing recent Chateau Mouton Rothschilds.

Wine & Dine E-Zine
www.winedine.co.uk/wine/auc1.html
Within the Wine & Dine E-Zine website is this article, by regular bidder Clifford Mould, about the tactics for successful buying at auction.

The German Wine Page
www.cogsci.ed.ac.uk/~peru/german_wine.html
The German Wine Page delivers what you would expect, such as advice on **Buying** and **Vintages**, as well as some relevant **Links**.

Channel Wine
www.channelwine.co.uk
Channel Wine is a network introducing the 'oenographiles' (wine label collectors) of France, Belgium and Switzerland. It is written in excellent English, providing you can cope with descriptions of wines as 'grandiose, athletic, sophisticated and indefatigable.' A flashing banner headline periodically appears with an exhortation to advertisers in horrifying *franglais*, 'Webissez vous!'

The Antique Wine Bottle and Black Glass Collectors Club

www.bankscon.freeserve.co.uk

The Antique Wine Bottle and Black Glass Collectors Club offers **Articles** (so far only four), **Archaeology** (two items), a **Bulletin Board** where collectors can post details of wants, an **Events** list, a **Directory of Links** to half a dozen other websites for bottle collectors, a **Photo Gallery** of a dozen images and **Curiosity Corner. Introduction for New Collectors**, though, is the best starting point on a first visit.

Taste of the Vine

www.tasteofthevine.co.uk

Taste of the Vine has had the bright idea that wine events, tours, treasure hunts and the like can form part of a corporate entertainment portfolio. Team-building events, for example, include **Interactive Cocktails** and **Whose Wine is it Anyway?** but there are many other possibilities, involvement in which would certainly contribute to any wine-buff's knowledge.

Wine Online

www.wineonline.co.uk

This is a final one to explore, especially if you are interested in wine tastings and similar events.

writing accessories

Last but not least, we come to writing accessories. Pens and pencils are, of course, what immediately come to mind, but other items like blotters, seals and inkwells are also avidly sought by collectors. Certain types of pen, indeed, are now very valuable. Also already much collected are typewriters, as will be seen from the two websites listed at the end of this section.

http://angelfire.com/fl/prestonthepenman			
Penman's Fountain Pen Site			
Overall rating: ★ ★ ★ ★			
Classification: Writing		**Readability:**	★ ★ ★ ★
Updating: Regular		**Reliability:**	★ ★ ★ ★
Navigation: ★ ★		**Speed:**	★ ★ ★
US			

This American website was being redesigned at the time of writing so the homepage was distinctly plain, but it is still the best source available.

SPECIAL FEATURES

Pen Jargon and Terms is a useful glossary explaining terms like 'blow filler', 'cracked ice' and 'spear feed.' The totally indispensable part of the website is found in the **Links,** the largest such list on the web. At the moment, these are listed by name alone, with no indication of what each website covers, but presumably this will change as the website is reborn. At the top of this page are some other internal links, to **Penman Monthly,** the online newsletter, and **Pen News.**

Pen Guide is a useful short article with some tips on caring for pens. **Penman's Openion** (*sic*) is an amusing description of the typical pen-hunter by Patrick Ramacker.

This will presumably alter considerably in appearance soon, so this description can hardly be very accurate nor can the star-rating be certain, but it is already a good website and should get even better.

OTHER SITES OF INTEREST

pens

Old Pens
www.old-pens.co.uk
David Wells has a personal website here with a particular interest in the British make, Conway Stewart.

Penfriend
www.penfriend.co.uk
Penfriend claims to be 'the World's largest independent fountain pen restorer.' There are three shops, all in London, from which they sell pens too.

Autographica
www.autographica.co.uk
The World's Largest Autograph Show, Autographica (see also p.60) has a **Lotsa-links** button from which you can access a **History of Pens** feature. This is a lengthy, genuinely informative article.

typewriters

The Classic Typewriter Page
http://xavier.xu.edu:8000/~polt/typewriters.html
The Classic Typewriter Page is headed by a picture of the charming Flying Oliver, and this whole website is a veritable box of delights for typewriter enthusiasts. The homepage is so clear and straightforward that no special instruction is needed here. Just click and go. Richard Polt is the US-based typewriter 'eccentric' and sometime cartoonist in charge.

How to Collect Antique Typewriters
www.etedeschi.ndirect.co.uk/howto4.htm
Richard Polt is also the author of this webpage, How to Collect Antique Typewriters.

Glossary of Internet Terms

Accelerators Add-on programs, which speed up browsing.

Acceptable Use Policy These are the terms and conditions of using the internet. They are usually set by organisations, who wish to regulate an individual's use of the internet. For example, an employer might issue a ruling on the type of email which can be sent from an office.

Access Provider A company which provides access to the internet, usually via a dial-up account. Many companies such as AOL and Dircon charge for this service, although there are an increasing number of free services such as Freeserve, Lineone and Tesco.net. Also known as an Internet Service Provider.

Account A user's internet connection, with an Access/Internet Service Provider, which usually has to be paid for.

Acrobat Reader Small freely-available program, or web browser plug-in, which lets you view a Portable Document Format (PDF) file.

Across Lite Plug-in which allows you to complete crossword puzzles online.

Address Location name for email or internet site, which is the online equivalent of a postal address. It is usually composed of a unique series of words and punctuation, such as *my.name@house.co.uk*. See also URL.

America Online (AOL) The world's most heavily subscribed online service provider.

Animated GIF Low-grade animation technique used on websites.

ASCII Stands for American Standard Code for Information Interchange. ASCII is a coding standard which all computers can recognise, ensuring that if a character is entered on one part of the internet, the same character will be seen elsewhere.

ASCII Art Art made of letters and other symbols. Because it is made up of simple text, it can be recognised by different computers.

ASDL Stands for Asynchronous Digital Subscriber Line, which is a high-speed copper wire allowing for the rapid transfer of information. Not widely in use at moment, though the government is pushing for its early introduction.

Attachment A file included with an email, which may be composed of text, graphics and sound. Attachments are encoded for transfer across the internet, and can be viewed in their original form by the recipient. An attachment is the equivalent of putting a photograph with a letter in the post.

Bookmark A function of the Netscape Navigator browser which allows you to save a link to your favourite sites, so that you can return straight there later without re-entering the address. Favorites in Internet Explorer is the same thing.

BPS Abbreviation of Bits Per Second, which is a measure of the speed at which information is transferred or downloaded.

Broadband A type of data transfer medium (usually a cable or wire) which can carry several signals at the same time. Most existing data transfer media are narrowband, and can only carry one signal at a time.

Browse Common term for looking around the web. See also Surfing.

Browser A generic term for the software that allows users to move and look around the Web. Netscape Navigator and Internet Explorer are the ones that most people are familiar with, accounting for 97 per cent of web hits.

Bulletin Board Service A BBS is a computer with a telephone connection, which allows you direct contact to upload and download information and converse with other users, via the computer. It was the forerunner to the online services and virtual communities of today.

Cache A temporary storage space on the hard drive of your computer, which stores downloaded websites. When you return to a website, information is retrieved from the cache and displayed much more rapidly. However, this information may not be the most recent version for sites which are frequently updated, and you will need to reload the website address for these.

Chat Talking to other users on the web in real time, but with typed instead of spoken words. Special software such as ICQ or MIRC is required before you can chat.

Chat Room An internet channel which allows several people to type in their messages, and talk to one another over the internet.

Clickstream The trail left as you 'click' your way around the web.

Codec Any technology which can compress/decompress data, such as MPEG and MP3.

Content The material on a website that actually relates to the site, and is hopefully of interest or value. Things like adverts are not considered to be part of the content. The term is also used to refer to information on the internet that can be seen by users, as opposed to programming and other background information.

Cookie A cookie is a nugget of information sometimes sent by websites to your hard drive when you visit. They contain such details as what you looked at and what you ordered, and can also add more information, so that the website can be customised to suit you.

Cybercafe Cafe where you can use a computer terminal to browse the net for a small fee.

Cyberspace When first coined by the sci-fi author William Gibson, it meant a shared hallucination which occurred when people logged on to computer networks. Now, it refers to the virtual space you're in when on the internet.

Dial Up A temporary telephone connection to your ISP's computer and how you make contact with your ISP, each time you log onto the Internet.

Domain The part of an Internet address which identifies an individual computer, and can often be a business or person's name. For example, in the www.goodwebguide.com the domain name is theGoodWebGuide.

Download Transfer of information from an Internet server to your computer.

Dynamic HTML The most recent version of the HTML standard.

Ecash Electronic cash, used to make transactions on the internet.

Ecommerce The name for business which is carried out over the internet.

Email Mail which is delivered electronically over the internet. Usually comprised of text messages, but can contain illustrations, music and animations. Mail is sent to an email address: the internet equivalent of a postal address.

Encryption A process whereby information is scrambled to produce a 'coded message', so that it can't be read while in transit on the internet. The recipient must have decryption software in order to read the message.

Expire Term referring to newsgroup postings which are automatically deleted after a fixed period of time.

Ezine Publication on the web, which is updated regularly.

FAQ Stands for frequently asked questions and is a common section on websites where the most common enquiries and their answers are archived.

Frame A method which splits web pages into several windows.

FTP/File Transfer Protocol Standard method for transporting files across the internet.

GIF/Graphics Interchange Format A format in which graphics are compressed, and a popular method of putting images onto the internet, as they take little time to download.

Gopher The gopher was the precursor of the world wide web. It consisted of archives accessed through a menu, usually organised by subject.

GUI/Graphical User Interface. This is the system which turns binary information into the words-and-images format you can see on your computer screen. For example, instead of seeing the computer language which denotes the presence of your toolbar, you actually see a toolbar.

Hackers A term which is used to refer to expert programmers who use their skills to break into computer systems, just for the fun of it. Nowadays, the word is more commonly associated with computer criminals, or Crackers.

Header Basic indication of what's in an email: who it's from, when it was sent, and what it's about.

Hit When a file is downloaded from a website it is referred to as a 'hit'. Measuring the number of hits is a rough method of counting how many people visit a website. Not wholly accurate as one website can contain many files, so one visit may generate several hits.

Homepage Usually associated with a personal site, but also refers to the first page on your browser, or the first page of a website.

Host Computer on which a website is stored. A host computer may store several websites, and usually has a fast, powerful connection to the internet. Also sometimes known as a Server.

HTML/Hypertext Mark-Up Language The computer code used to construct web pages.

HTTP/Hypertext Transfer Protocol The protocol for moving HTML files across the web.

Hyperlink A word or graphic formatted so that when you click on it, you move from one area to another. See also hypertext.

Hypertext Text within a document which is formatted so that it acts as a link from one page to another, or from one document to another.

Image Map A graphic which contains hyperlinks.

Interface What you actually see on your computer screen.

Internet One or more computers connected to one another is an internet (lower case i). The Internet is the biggest of all the internets, consisting of a worldwide collection of interconnected computer networks.

Internet Explorer One of the most popular pieces of browser software, produced by Microsoft.

Intranet A network of computers, which works in the same way as an internet, but for internal use, such as within a corporation.

ISDN/Integrated Services Digital Network Digital telephone line which facilitates very fast connections and can transfer large amounts of data. It can carry more than one form of data at once.

ISP/Internet Service Provider See Access Provider.

Java Programming language which can be used to create interactive multimedia effects on webpages. The language is used to create programmes known as *applets* that add features such as animations, sound and even games to websites.

JavaScript A scripting language which, like Java, can be used to add extra multimedia features. However, in contrast with Java it does not consist of separate programmes. JavaScript is embedded into the HTML text and can be interpreted by the browser, provided that the user has a JavaScript enabled browser.

JPEG Stands for 'Joint Photographic Experts Group' and is the name given to a type of format which compresses photos, so that they can be seen on the web.

Kill file A function which allows a user to block incoming information from unwanted sources. Normally used on email and newsreaders.

LAN/Local Area Network A type of internet, but limited to a single area, such as an office.

Login The account name or password needed to access a computer system.

Link Connection between web pages, or one web document and another, which are accessed via formatted text and graphic.

Mailing List A discussion group which is associated with a website. Participants send their emails to the site, and it is copied and sent by the server to other individuals on the mailing list.

Modem A device for converting digital data into analogue signals for transmission along standard phone lines. The usual way for home users to connect to the internet or log into their email accounts. May be internal (built into the computer) or external (a desk-top box connected to the computer).

MP3 A compressed music file format, which has almost no loss of quality although the compression rate may be very high.

Netiquette Guidelines for polite behaviour when exchanging information with people on the net.

Netscape Popular browser, now owned by AOL.

Newbie Term for someone new to the Internet. Used pejoratively of newcomers to bulletin boards or chat, who commit the sin of asking obvious questions or failing to observe the netiquette.

Newsgroup Discussion group among Internet users who share an interest. There are thousands of newsgroups covering every possible subject.

Offline Not connected to the internet, therefore saving telephone charges if you connect through a telephone line.

Online Connected to the internet.

Offline Browsing A function of the browser software, which allows the user to download pages and read them while offline.

Online Service Provider Similar to an access provider, but provides additional features such as live chat.

PDF/Portable Document Format A file format created by Adobe for offline reading of brochures, reports and other documents with complex graphic design, which can be read by anyone with Acrobat Reader.

Plug-in Piece of software which adds functions (such as playing music or video) to another, larger software program.

POP3/Post Office Protocol An email protocol that allows you to pick up your mail from any location on the web.

Portal A website which offers many services, such as search engines, email and chat rooms, and to which people are likely to return to often. ISPs such as Yahoo and Alta Vista provide portal sites which are the first thing you see when you log on, and, in theory, act as gateways to the rest of the web.

Post/Posting Information sent to a usenet group, bulletin board, message board or by email.

PPP/Point to Point Protocol The agreed way of sending data over dial-up connections, so that the user's computer, the modem and the internet server can all recognise it. It is the protocol which allows you to get online.

Protocol Convention detailing a set of actions that computers in a network must follow so that they can understand one another.

Query Request for specific information from a database.

RAM/Random Access Memory Your computer's short-term memory.

RealPlayer A plug-in program that allows you to view video in real-time and listen to sound. RealPlayer is becoming increasingly important for web use.

Router An interface between two networks that decides how to route information.

Searchable Database A database on a website which allows the user to search for information, usually by keyword.

Search Engine Programs which enable web users to search for pages and sites using keywords. They are usually to be found on portal sites and browser homepages. Infoseek, Alta Vista and Lycos are popular search engines.

Secure Transactions Information transfers which are encrypted so that only the sender and recipient have access to the uncoded message, keeping the details within private. The term is most commonly used to refer to credit card transactions, although other information can be sent in a secure form.

Server A powerful computer that has a permanent, fast connection to the internet. Such computers are usually owned by companies and act as host computers for websites.

Sign-on To connect to the internet and start using one of its facilities.

Shareware Software that doesn't have to be paid for or test version of software that the user can access for free, as a trial before buying it.

Skins Simple software that allows the user to change the appearance of an application.

Standard A style which the whole of the computer industry has agreed upon. Industry standards mean that hardware and software produced by the various different computer companies will work with one another.

Stream A technique for processing data, which enables it to be downloaded as a continuous stream, and viewed or listened to as the data arrives.

Surfing Slang for looking around the Internet, without any particular aim, following links from site to site.

TLA/Three Letter Acronyms Netspeak for the abbreviations of net jargon, such as BPS (Bits Per Second) and ISP (Internet Service Provider).

Upload To send files from your computer to another one on the internet. When you send an email you are uploading a file.

URL/Uniform Resource Locator Jargon for an address on the internet, such as www.thegoodwebguide.co.uk.

Usenet A network of newsgroups, which form a worldwide system, on which anyone can post 'news'.

Virtual Community Name given to a congregation of regular mailing list/newsgroup users.

VRML/Virtual Reality Modeling Language Method for creating 3D environments on the web.

Wallpaper Description of the sometimes hectic background patterns which appear behind the text on some websites.

Web Based Email/Webmail Email accounts such as Hotmail and Rocketmail, accessed via an Internet browser rather than an email program such as Outlook Express. Webmail has to be typed while the user is online, but can be accessed from anywhere on the Web.

Webmaster A person responsible for a web server. May also be known as System Administrator.

Web Page Document which forms one part of a website (though some sites are a single page), usually formatted in HTML.

Web Ring Loose association of websites which are usually dedicated to the same subject and often contain links to one another.

Website A collection of related web pages which often belong to an individual or organisation and are about the same subject.

World Wide Web The part of the Internet which is easy to get around and see. The term is often mistakenly interchanged with Internet, though the two are not the same. If the Internet is a shopping mall, with shops, depots, and delivery bays, then the web is the actual shops which the customers see and use.

Index

The Good Web Guide
www.thegoodwebguide.co.uk

The Good Web Guide provides simple one-click access to all the sites mentioned in this book, and is an easy way to start exploring the internet. All books about the internet become slightly out of date as soon they're printed, but with the free updates you'll receive as a subscriber to the Good Web Guide website, this book will remain current as long as you're a member.

The goodwebguide.co.uk homepage provides links to each of the GWG subject channels, including Antiques and Collectibles. It also lists headlines and links to some of the newest articles, reviews and competitions on the site, and details of special offers on other Good Web Guide books.

you've filled in and submitted your details a menu will appear on the left of the page. Choose the option Register a Purchase. A list of questions will appear, but you only need to answer the one relevant to this book, and you will need to have the book in front of you to find the answer. Once you're registered you'll be able to view the contents of this book online, and be eligible for free updates. As a member you can upgrade to obtain access to all the channels at a specially discounted rate.

Reviews are organised by chapter, with the new reviews in the Latest Additions section. At the bottom of each review there is a link straight to the site, so you don't have to worry about typing in the addresses. New reviews are added at least monthly, sometimes weekly. You can also sign up for monthly free newsletters to have website reviews delivered straight to your desk.

Although some reviews and articles are free to view, the majority of the content on the Good Web Guide site is accessible only to members. Begin by clicking on the small 'Register Now' icon near the top left of the page. When